SOURDOUGH REINVENTED

WILD BREAD

FLOUR + WATER + AIR

MaryJane Butters

Owner of the 1890
Historic Barron Flour Mill

SOURDOUGH REINVENTED

WILD BREAD

FLOUR + WATER + AIR

MaryJane Butters

Owner of the 1890
Historic Barron Flour Mill

GIBBS SMITH
TO ENRICH AND INSPIRE HUMANKIND

First Edition
22 21 20   5

Text, illustrations, and photographs copyright © 2018 MaryJane Butters except for historical photos.

Published by
Gibbs Smith
P.O. Box 667
Layton, Utah 84041

1.800.835.4993 orders
Gibbs-Smith.com

Printed and bound in China.

Gibbs Smith books are printed on either recycled, 100% post-consumer waste; FSC-certified papers; or on paper produced from sustainable PEFC-certified forest/controlled wood sources. Learn more at PEFC.org.

ISBN: 978-1-4236-4818-5
Library of Congress Control Number: 2017950586

Questions? Comments? Join our network of home and professional bakers at **WildBread.net**, where all things wild bread are discussed and book updates are noted.

D E D I C A T I O N

Joseph Barron Jr.

This book is a tribute to

the three generations of men and women who,
by industry and thrift, built and ran the historic
1890 four-story Barron Flour Mill that is
now under my care and ownership.

Moses Barron, 1829–1905, grain miller
Joseph Barron Sr., 1866–1955, grain miller
Joseph Barron Jr., 1909–2000, grain miller
MaryJane Butters, 1953–, grain miller/
                 organic farmer/dairy owner

66 Bread deals with
living things, with
giving life, with
growth, with the
seed, the grain that
nurtures us. It's
not coincidence that
we say bread is the
staff of life. 99

– Lionel Poilâne

CONTENTS

Quick-and-easy treats, everything from panbread bites to muffins to pancakes to doughnuts.

White Wheat

Einkorn (heirloom wheat)

Bread-Machine Kamut
(heirloom whole wheat)

White Wheat

8

White Rice (gluten free)

Quinoa (gluten free)

Find it, buy it! Not all equipment, cookware, and tools are created equal. Lean in for the lowdown. Also, gift ideas.

Quinoa (gluten free)

Millers Joseph Barron Jr. and MaryJane Butters, 1997

When I first launched my idea for wild-yeast "Bread the MaryJane Way" in 2008 for my magazine, I never dreamed readers would respond with such rise! What I didn't know back then was that once they brought my idea into their kitchens, I'd end up with some 2,000 incredibly useful comments and questions on my chatroom.

"I have a question. I live in Texas, and right now the weather is jumping up and down (lows in 30s, highs in 60s–70s). Will that affect my starter? I live in an older house (very drafty) and my stove is right by the back door, so I can't leave it in the kitchen area. Maybe a bedroom on the south side of the house might work (away from windows)???"

And the reader who answered her ...

"SUCCESS!! I got it right! Yaaaaaay! This is what I did: I followed all the directions exactly as MaryJane said in her magazine. The first rise was ho-hum and about six hours long. For the second rise, I put it in a casserole dish and put it on a heating pad (like for back pain) with a damp towel over it and let it rise until it truly was doubled in bulk, which took about six hours. The lack of moisture in the air and cooler temperatures really do make wintertime bread making a little trickier. Anyway, I popped it in the oven, and PERFECTION!"

All THAT led to THIS. A book.

What I know now is that I can take my idea for a simple, olde-world starter (mother) and turn it into a formula to satisfy most every personality type on Earth. I can break bread with white flour only eaters (in honor of my Wonder-Bread-only, I might die tomorrow father-in-law, who lived to age 98), and I can offer bread to above it all, uncompromising purists by serving up a lofty loaf using 100 percent heirloom grains. And I can bake a loaf of bread that rises to the rafters for those who believe it's best to sprout their grains first. I can serve up a soft, skyward loaf of I can't believe this is gluten-free rice or quinoa-only bread for those who are gluten free. And for those needing instant gratification, my pancakes, waffles, muffins, panbread bites, and even chocolate cake satisfy that I want something sourdough now urge.

Welcome and come on in. Have I got a bread for you!

P R E F A C E

I was born to crave and love good flour, bred to love bread, destined to fall for Joseph Barron Jr., "the town miller," and eventually take over stewardship of his family's legacy—one that started two generations prior, back in 1862 in Barronvale, Pennsylvania, with Moses Barron, his grandfather.

Joseph Jr. got a deferment during World War II to continue the important work of providing food to civilians.

Calendars that pre-date World War I still decorate the office walls inside the old four-story mill, above the original typewriter and safe.

For the three years we worked together milling grains (1995–1998), Joseph Barron Jr., in his late 80s, started to wear out, but he was still bending right to the floor to grab 50-pound sacks of flour and hoist them up onto his right shoulder. (His posture was impeccably straight and erect.) But it tugged at my heartstrings to see how they weighed down his small and diminishing frame. Maybe it was that left-handed, loving bottom pat he always gave the sack once it settled onto his shoulder. Maybe it was the way he taught me to test for gluten (protein) by slowly chewing on a mouthful of hard red winter-wheat berries: The more it resembled bubble gum after 15 minutes of chewing, the higher the gluten content. "Good for bread, then," he'd say. "My bakers will love it." And they did.

After Joseph lost his beloved wife, Ethel, the local women who loved his flour returned the favor, coming almost daily to bring him their little creations—"a bit of extra, no big deal." But I knew they were vying for his approval, something hard to come by. I brought him baked goods, too. But when Joseph put his Old Mill up for sale, I baked up a plan that involved a state-funded rural rehabilitation loan. Sifting through dozens of prospective buyers as carefully as he sifted different kinds of grain, in the end he announced,

"I think you'll do."

Barron Flour Mill

Moscow–Pullman Daily News, Oct. 3 & 4, 1998: "Nick Ogle, MaryJane Butters, and Joseph Barron pose outside the Oakesdale Mill for a family photo of sorts. Barron has passed the tradition of milling on to Butters and Ogle. The two will continue serving small farmers and their organic crops in the same style Barron did years ago. Scenes from both the new and old mill are rich with history. From Barron's honor-system sign, to yesteryear's tools lit by beaming sunlight, both mills and millers have tales to tell and flour to make."

During the years I worked alongside Joseph, I ate more than my fill of his frugal bachelor food—things like Spam and Velveeta cheese—but one day, he called just before I was about to leave my farm for the 60-minute drive to his place, where I'd planned to spend the day milling the grains and legumes I'd need for the dry mixes I sold mail-order. "MaryJane, I'm not feeling well. Do you have any dandelion greens you can bring me? My mother fed me dandelion greens whenever I felt bad, but I've sprayed all of mine."

That afternoon, Joe and I shared a bowl of bitter greens, him telling me stories about the backyard cow he milked. "Fresh milk straight from the teat—now there's medicine."

Joseph, born in 1909 in a living area attached to the Old Mill, followed in the footsteps of his father and grandfather before him by milling grains his entire working life, for 70-plus years, feeding the farmers of the Palouse region of northeast Washington and northwest Idaho and their livestock. There were three blacksmiths, three railroads, a jeweler, and a cobbler in Oakesdale back then. Young Joseph grew up to the sound of hammers and anvils in a town that was thriving.

But as farming became more mechanized, his market for the cracked grains fed to family cows, pigs, and outback chickens dropped off. People started buying their meat, eggs, and flour in grocery stores. Larger mills were rapidly taking over markets for brands like the centuries-old Barron flour known as "Sweet Home."

The 19 flour mills that once graced the area slowly died one by one.

But the Barrons held on.

Joseph had gone to work for his father right out of high school, in 1927. They survived the Great Depression by cleaning seed, storing grain, and selling coal.

The Spokesman Review, January 6, 1998

Mill on the Palouse

History grinds on

New generation of millers takes over a wholesome tradition

Mill: Sifted through prospective buyers

Clipboards with farmers' names scrawled in pencil still hang above the bins alongside knot-free handrails, worn smooth. Exquisite machines fill all four floors, handmade in the manner and style of heirloom violins or grand pianos— treasured artifacts from an era when time was plentiful and people poured their artisan hearts into the making of everyday tools.

The Old Mill produced flour until 1960, when Joseph Jr. closed the doors once and for all. He worked for a while in a nearby corporate grain co-op, but in survivor fashion, returned to his trade by using a unique set of mill blueprints engineered by an English businessman who lost his mill during World War II as a result of bombing raids.

In a garage-type building across the creek from the Old Mill and behind his house, he opened up for business again, this time milling organic grains, a new market that showed promise.

The Barron Flour Mill in its heyday.

Employing the Englishman's unique design that uses centrifugal force at more than 3,500 revolutions per minute, the mill explodes grains rather than crushing them. Small enough to fit easily in the back of a pickup truck, it can mill 500 pounds of grain per hour. The old four-story mill could do only 88.

With his new mill, new flour, and new market, Joseph created an almost cult-like following of bakers. His milling process produced whole-wheat flour so fine it performed more like white flour. (Think brown talcum powder.) Standard whole-wheat mills oftentimes add moisture to soften wheat, causing it to go rancid faster. Joseph's mill doesn't require the addition of moisture and also does the job at a lower temperature, both of which result in a longer shelf life for flour. Joseph had the nearby university test his flour. His whole-wheat flour, when stored at moderate temperatures, did not develop rancidity for at least two years.

During the early years of his new mill, he sold his products under the trade name "Nutri Grain"—until the Kellogg Company talked him out of it. Needing cash, he sold them the name in 1980 and began selling his products under the name "Joseph's."

When the sale of his Old Mill to me (along with his new little unique mill) made the local newspaper, they got two sentences out of him.

"Never lost the place," he said.

"Never lost it."

The Barron Flour Mill is a fitting tribute to a man who still occupies the memories of those who knew him, reminding us to honor the grit, grace, and resilience of those whose work provides us our daily bread.

For the decades that Joseph sold flour, he offered it self-serve, just in case someone stopped by and he wasn't around, "If no one here, serve yourself."

He kept the drawer below the sign full of change, claiming no one ever helped themselves to the money.

BEGINNER BREADS

In This Section

*includes gluten-free versions

20

Beginner Dutch-Oven Bread, p. 46

In this section (that you can't skip over), I'll show you how to create a wild-yeast starter or "MOTHER." My technique uses airborne yeasts and probiotic-friendly lactic-acid bacteria that exist naturally around us in the air we breathe. Some of it can also be found on the surface of grains. The yeasts give rise to breads naturally, without commercial yeast or chemical rising agents. It's a 5,000-year-old bread-making method that eliminates the need for modern store-bought yeast. Baking bread using the healthy "critters" that are familiar to your body from the air that surrounds you, rather than only one variety of mass-produced yeast singled out, is like the difference between the diversity of a rainforest and a tree farm.

Not only that, but bread made using wild yeasts enhances your immune system. Phytic acid (called the anti-nutrient) in grain needs to be neutralized in order for the nutrients present to be more readily absorbed by the human body. In naturally leavened bread, phytic acid is neutralized because of the slow fermentation that takes place. But in commercial, quick-rise, yeasted breads, as much as 90 percent remains, depending on the grain and whether or not it's whole versus processed. Furthermore, the resulting phytates reduce the digestibility of starches, proteins, and fats. By contrast, in naturally leavened breads, complex carbohydrates are broken down into more digestible simple sugars and protein is broken down into absorbable amino acids so that your body has access to these vital, life-giving nutrients. In addition, the lactic acid bacteria lowers the glycemic index of bread, making it better for people who are challenged by diabetes or watching their weight. In other words, that bagel you've been thinking about is more like a vitamin pill than a source of guilt.

During the time it takes to get your mother established (at least one month), you'll feed your kitchen "COUNTER MOTHER" flour and water 2x/day (takes less than a minute). And once a week, you'll bake breads with a traditional *sour* sourdough flavor (or make yummy pancakes and waffles). During this time, her alchemy will come into balance as she continues to pull wild yeasts from the air, strengthening her ability to eventually give a lofty rise to an endless variety of breads.

Once your mother is fully mature and you're ready to dig into the Advanced Section (p. 56), I'll show you how to maintain your mother in your refrigerator. Your "REFRIGERATOR MOTHER" will only need weekly feedings and you can go as long as a month without using her to bake breads. I'll also teach you how to use your established Refrigerator Mother for baking breads that have less, if any, sourdough flavor. Once you've mastered wild-yeast bread making, you'll love the way wild breads loft with wild abandon.

Before you get started, make sure you're able to commit to 1 minute 2x/day feedings for at least a month, as well as the time needed for once per week "Bake Days."

The fine print...
During the time you have your mother living on your counter and you decide to make a batch of bread using store-bought yeast or you bring store-bought yeasted breads into your home, your mother will get out of sorts. In fact, she may never get over your transgression. If you bring breads made with commercial yeast into your home, you can cover your mother in her glass container and keep her in your refrigerator until the coast is clear.

If you have questions along the way (or merely need a place to show off your successes), go to WildBread.net and join in on the discussion.

But first,

the men and women of my historic flour mill left their mark on our lives in countless ways. Specifically, the women left wallpaper, layers upon layers. **Throughout my book,** I've incorporated **some of the patterns** I found. **The black background** you'll see throughout is the back side of a precious and **rare oversized piece of slate** that served as an **office blackboard.**

And,

one of the first things you encounter when you step back in time is the intense urge early pioneer women had to feminize their surroundings, everything from planting a lilac tree in front of a ramshackle, dirt-floor shelter to drawn-work in which they painstakingly pulled threads from flour-sack towels in order to create the look of lace. **I'm sure that within minutes of men inventing machinery to grind wheat, women thought "FLOUR PASTE" for hanging wallpaper.**

Joseph Barron Jr. and his mother

Now, let's get started ...

I love teaching beginners my super-simple **1 minute 2x/day, 5 minutes on Bake Day** wild-yeast method. Having launched my idea in 2008, I'm familiar with all the what-ifs and what-nots that trip people up. In every instance, it's an equipment, flour, or water-quality problem. Because I want you to be successful, you'll need to round up some equipment. You probably already have some of it on hand.

Here's what you'll need to get started:

Beginner Equipment ✓ List

- ☑ ONE 3.75-qt *Glasslock* mixing bowl (10 1/2"W x 5 1/2"H)

- ☐ ONE 10 1/2" *Marinex* baking dish

- ☐ TWO 2-qt *Pyrex* bakeware dishes with lids

- ☐ TWO 1.5-qt *Pyrex* sculpted loaf pans with covers (9"L x 5"W x 3"H)

- ☑ ONE 8-cup *Pyrex* measuring cup

- ☑ ONE 5- to 6-qt lidded cast-iron Dutch oven

- ☑ TWO 13" x 18" baker's sheets

- ☐ ONE lasagna trio pan

- ☑ ONE 1/8-cup coffee scoop

- ☑ TWO silicone spatulas (you can use wood, but they're going to see a lot of water, and that's hard on wood)

- ☑ ONE 12-PACK 28" x 28" flour-sack cotton towels

- ☑ ONE quick-read digital thermometer (for an instant, deluxe version, see Section 5, Equipment, p. 203)

- ☑ ONE 4-oz spray bottle

- ☑ ONE *Brød & Taylor* folding bread proofer and yogurt maker with shelf kit (proofer is optional, but highly recommended)*

Resources
*BrodAndTaylor.com

The fine print ...
This equipment list, along with basic kitchen equipment, will get you through the recipes in this section.

For a more detailed, itemized discussion, see Section 5, Equipment, p. 200.

Items listed are commonly available online (simply use the specific name provided for an online search) or check with your local kitchen store.

Now, all you need is at least 10 pounds of good ORGANIC flour and some purified water.

Sorry, but whenever I've tried non-organic flour or chlorinated tap water, weird things happened, like my wild-yeast starter would turn black (or gray or red) or it would get moldy. Trust me, I was determined to make *any-ole-flour* and *any-ole-water* work, because wouldn't that make my job a whole lot easier and my idea more universally accepted? You have to somehow find good water. If you don't have your own water from a well or spring (that's been tested for purity), **buy a couple of gallons of distilled water to get started** while you figure out how to purify your tap water (see Section 5, Equipment, p. 209).

To create a single-flour wild-yeast starter, aka mother, I came

up with eight different flour options (all of them organic and the best in their class). More about these flours and others in Section 4, Let's Talk Flour, p. 190.

Organic **White**-Wheat Flour (unbleached)
WildBread.net

Organic heirloom **Kamut**® (Khorasan) Whole-Wheat Flour
MontanaFlour.com

Organic **Sprouted** Whole-Wheat Flour
HealthyFlour.com (recipes were tested using Organic Sprouted Hard Red Wheat Flour)

Organic heirloom **Einkorn** Wheat Flour
JovialFoods.com

Organic heirloom **Einka**® (einkorn) Whole-Wheat Flour
BluebirdGrainFarms.com

Organic **White-Rice** Flour
BobsRedMill.com

Organic **Brown-Rice** Flour
EdenFoods.com
TrueFoodsMarket.com
BobsRedMill.com

Organic **Quinoa** Flour
(requires at-home milling) see Section 5, Equipment, p. 208

> My favorite to work with is **Kamut**. It's doughy but never sticky, and has a distinct buttery flavor. **Sprouted** is exquisitely nutty. **White** is lofty. **Einka** is primal (in a good way). **Rice** surprises: "This is *rice*?!" But, **Quinoa** knocks it out of the park.

WHITE   KAMUT   SPROUTED   EINKORN

Mother trials in our test kitchen.

Let me help you get all this heirloom stuff straight. Neither Khorasan nor einkorn are brands; they're varieties of wheat that have never been hybridized and are centuries old. Einka® and Kamut® are the trademarks of farmers who grow einkorn and Khorasan varieties of wheat, respectively.

Well then, why did I suggest both einkorn and Einka flours in my lineup, you ask? The company, Jovial, that sells einkorn flour (the wheat is grown in Italy) removes 80 percent of the germ and bran for a lighter flour that has a longer shelf life. Bluebird Grain Farms' Einka brand of flour is 100 percent whole-wheat einkorn and is grown in the U.S. For more about these heirloom varieties, including Khorasan, see Section 4, Let's Talk Flour, p. 190.

EINKA   WHITE RICE   BROWN RICE   QUINOA

The Mother of All Starters

Your *Glasslock* bowl, kept on the counter, is going to be the place the wild-yeast starter (your **Counter Mother**) lives. Pick a day of the week you're able to consistently bake bread and start your mother **in the morning** on that day. (Saturdays work well for most people.) Here's how to get started:

1. Pour 1/2" purified water into your 10 1/2" *Marinex* baking dish. Place a folded flour-sack cotton towel in the water. Set aside.

2. Using your 1/8-cup coffee scoop, put 3/8 cup organic flour and 1/4 cup purified water in your 3.75-qt *Glasslock* bowl. Stir thoroughly with a spatula until mixture is smooth and relatively free of lumps.

3. Now that you've started your mother, wring the water from your towel back into the baking dish, place your bowl inside the baking dish, and cover with the moist towel, tucking the edges down into the water in the baking dish. At all times going forward, you'll keep purified water in the baking dish so the water can wick up the towel to keep it moist (like a kerosene-lamp wick). **How long does stirring your mother and tucking her in take? Less than a minute, tops.**

Tip: Both the water and the flour used for bread making need to be at room temperature. We keep a week's worth of flour in a Progressive flour keeper with built-in leveler (p. 195) right next to our Counter Mother, along with a glass gallon jug of purified water.

4. **In the evening, repeat step 2 and tuck your mother in.**

Now, two times per day, every morning and evening thereafter for six days, you're going to stir in 3/8 cup more flour and 1/4 cup more purified water. Whip vigorously for about 30 seconds until mixture is smooth and relatively free of lumps. Check to make sure your baking dish still has plenty of purified water, and replace the flour-sack cotton towel with a clean towel at least once a week.

On the seventh day, it's time to bake. Your mother should be alive with bubbles and smell pleasantly sour—like stout beer. If you don't think she's ready for bread yet, turn to p. 174 and whip up a batch of pancakes. If you think she still needs another week after that, I'm sure she's up for some waffles, p. 176. **After two weeks of pancakes and waffles, she'll be ready for a batch of batter bread.**

No matter what you're making, **pour the entire mother into your 8-cup *Pyrex* measuring "bowl."** Wash the *Glasslock* bowl and *Marinex* baking dish. Remove 1/2 cup mother from the *Pyrex* measuring "bowl" and return it to your *Glasslock* bowl, feed your mother her breakfast: 3/8 cup flour and 1/4 cup purified water, and mix well—this will now be your mother that you'll feed 2x/day until your next Bake Day. Let her rest until evening, then feed her dinner: 3/8 cup flour and 1/4 cup purified water. You will continue this daily morning and evening routine until Bake Day the following week. The "activated batter" left in your *Pyrex* measuring "bowl" is for **Bake Day** (p. 32).

This is what you'll see first thing in the morning—a bubbly, very-much-alive mother.

First, you'll add flour.

Then water.

After that, you'll give her a good stir to mix the flour in thoroughly and properly aerate her (like us, she needs oxygen).

Once you've given her a stir, use a second spatula to clean the excess off your stir spatula. You know it was a mother who said, "Waste not, want not."

Tip: For mothers with a thinner consistency like einkorn and brown rice, mix in flour first, then add water. This will make it easier to achieve a smooth consistency. You'll want to do the opposite for thicker mothers like sprouted wheat and white rice. First mix in water, then add flour.

Love Your Mother

For the first month, your mother will live on your counter, right next to where you make your morning coffee and evening tea, so her 2x/day stir that takes less than a minute can be part of your daily kitchen routine. It's a lot like nurturing a house plant—she's very much alive and willing to thrive if loved. (Once you've moved into my Advanced Section, she'll live in your refrigerator and you'll feed her only once a week.)

But there's finesse to tucking her in each time you've added only the very best flour and water. Her towel not only needs to be kept moist, but it needs to be laundered using a non-toxic, eco-friendly laundry detergent (mainstream detergents are likely to impact the health of your mother). Speaking of non-toxic, make sure the environment of your home is free from things like perfume-emitting air fresheners and overly toxic cleaning supplies.

Your mother will do best in a 70–73°F environment. Higher temps only make her more active. But cooler temps aren't her thing. The solution? The *Brød & Taylor* Bread Proofer and Yogurt Maker (see Section 5, Equipment, p. 209). If your home is chilly, you can easily keep her alive and well by letting her live inside the proofer set at a temperature somewhere between 70–73°F. And when it comes time to let your breads rise, you'll regard your proofer as one of your most prized possessions.

hankie pocket

In the early 1940s, an estimated three million farm women and children were wearing flour-sack garments.

Reaching their peak of popularity in the '50s, about 50 million flour sacks were sold yearly, full of flour, and then recycled by women into incredible ornate aprons, pillowcases, quilts, tablecloths, stuffed toys, dolls, everyday apparel, even underwear and wedding dresses.

I thought I'd won the lottery when a friend gifted me the flour-sack apron pictured here that she'd come across in a secondhand store. Using it as a template, I turned it into a one-size-fits-most pattern (embroidery template included), available at WildBread.net.

It's Bake Day. You've been feeding and nurturing your Counter Mother all week, and per the instructions on p. 28, you're going to put your entire mother* into your 8-cup *Pyrex* "bowl," wash your *Glasslock* bowl and *Marinex* baking dish, remove 1/2 cup mother from your "bowl" and return it to your clean bowl/baking dish setup, feed your mother breakfast: 3/8 cup flour and 1/4 cup water, and stir/cover. This is now your mother that you'll feed 2x/day until your next Bake Day. The "activated batter" left in your *Pyrex* "bowl" is now ready to be turned into oven-fresh bread in time for your evening meal.

Very generously butter your two 2-qt *Pyrex* bakeware dishes (you'll use about 2 T softened butter for each bakeware dish) and dust with flour; set aside. To your batter, add honey and salt and stir well. (The honey sweetens the rise—I know it seems like a small amount, but it makes a big difference.) If you're making white-rice bread, also note that you'll add water.

Depending on the type of flour you're using and the volume of batter in your 8-cup "bowl," you'll need to add varied amounts of flour to reach the desired consistency for baking. Start with the smallest amount of your chosen flour in the chart below and add incrementally until the batter is the consistency of softened cream cheese.

	Activated Batter	Honey	Salt	Water	Flour (same type as mother)
White	6–7 cups	2 t	1 t	none	2–2 1/2 cups
Kamut	5 1/2–6 1/2 cups	2 t	1 t	none	1/4–3/4 cup
Sprouted	5 1/2–6 1/2 cups	2 t	1 t	none	3/4–1 1/4 cups
Einkorn	6–7 cups	2 t	1 t	none	3–3 1/2 cups
Einka	5 1/2–6 1/2 cups	2 t	1 t	none	2 1/4–2 3/4 cups
White Rice	6–7 cups	2 t	1 t	3/4 cup	1/2–1 cup
Brown Rice	5 1/2–6 1/2 cups	2 t	1 t	none	3/4–1 1/4 cups
Quinoa	4 1/2–5 1/2 cups	2 t	1 t	none	2 1/4–2 3/4 cups

*Volume of mother will vary from week to week. Precision during feedings will help keep the volume consistent, but the bubbles inside the mother will also impact the final volume measurement.

After the batter is mixed, divide it evenly between your two prepared *Pyrex* bakeware dishes. Flatten the tops of the loaves with a spatula and brush them with melted butter. Put the lids on (cocked ever so slightly to one side so the bread can breathe), set aside in a warm place (70–73°F), and **wait 6–8 hours** or until the dough is level with the top of your bakeware dish (rice breads will be down 1/2" to 1" from the top). You can hasten the process by using a proofer with shelf kit set to 85°F. If using a proofer, you won't need to cover the dishes with their lids, but you will need to fill the water tray.

Preheat oven to 425°F. **Bake** loaves on lowest oven rack for **25–30 minutes** or until bread is nicely browned and internal temperature reaches 200–205°F. **Bake rice breads** on lowest oven rack for **40 minutes** (this will give you a nice, crisp crust), or until internal temperature reaches 200–205°F. Remove from oven and tip loaves out onto a cooling rack (this will keep your crust crisp on all sides).

Please note: Rather than list butter or safflower oil for bakeware prep as an ingredient in our recipe charts, you'll need to have a ready supply of both on hand.

Einkorn

Tip: To brown the surface of white- or brown-rice batter-bread loaves (quinoa browns beautifully on its own), dissolve 1/2 t baking soda in 1/4 cup water. Transfer to a spray bottle and mist tops of loaves halfway through baking.

Now you know why I recommend an 8-cup *Pyrex* measuring "bowl," because it also serves as your mixing bowl—perfect for mixing because you can hold onto the handle while giving the contents a good stir.

Einka

Divide batter evenly between two prepared bakeware dishes.

You'll see bubbles on the surface within the first 1–2 hours.

It's ready to bake when dough is level with the top (rice breads will be down 1/2" to 1" from the top).

Why bake an artisan-style round loaf in a glass dish? One word: crust. Not only is the crust amazing, but the inside is perfectly moist. It's the kind of loaf you tear apart with your hands and afterward can't believe you ate the whole thing. My straight-up farmer husband loves all eight varieties, but he especially loves the white-rice version: "It's the crust that slays me." I also chose this method because breads made with a young wild-yeast starter require a 6–8 hour rise, so I needed a way for the bread to stay moist during its rise. Hence, a lidded bakeware dish. And **I wanted your first loaf to be super-simple.** You don't even get your hands dirty because the batter goes directly from your 8-cup "bowl" into your bakeware dish.

With this method, **you can come home from work, pop it in the oven, and have bread for dinner without any muss or fuss at all.**

Einka

White

Kamut

Size of Floor Op

Fig. G

Sprouted

Einkorn

It's Bake Day. You've been feeding and nurturing your Counter Mother all week, and per the instructions on p. 28, you're going to put your entire mother* into your 8-cup *Pyrex* "bowl," wash your *Glasslock* bowl and *Marinex* baking dish, remove 1/2 cup mother from your "bowl" and return it to your clean bowl/baking dish setup, feed your mother breakfast: 3/8 cup flour and 1/4 cup water, and stir/cover. This is now your mother that you'll feed 2x/day until your next Bake Day. The "activated batter" left in your *Pyrex* "bowl" is now ready to be turned into oven-fresh bread in time for your evening meal.

Very generously butter your two 1.5-qt *Pyrex* loaf pans (you'll use about 2 T softened butter for each loaf pan) and dust with flour; set aside. To your batter, add honey and salt and stir well. (The honey sweetens the rise—I know it seems like a small amount, but it makes a big difference.) If you're making rice breads, also note that you'll add water to white rice, and eggs to both white and brown rice.

Depending on the type of flour you're using and the volume of batter in your 8-cup "bowl," you'll need to add varied amounts of flour to reach the desired consistency for baking. Start with the smallest amount of your chosen flour in the chart below and add incrementally until the batter is the consistency of softened cream cheese.

	Activated Batter	Honey	Salt	Water	Eggs	Flour (same type as mother)
White	6–7 cups	2 t	1 t	none	none	2–2 1/2 cups
Kamut	5 1/2–6 1/2 cups	2 t	1 t	none	none	1/4–3/4 cup
Sprouted	5 1/2–6 1/2 cups	2 t	1 t	none	none	3/4–1 1/4 cups
Einkorn	6–7 cups	2 t	1 t	none	none	3–3 1/2 cups
Einka	5 1/2–6 1/2 cups	2 t	1 t	none	none	2 1/4–2 3/4 cups
White Rice	6–7 cups	2 t	1 t	1/2 cup	4	3/4–1 1/4 cups
Brown Rice	5 1/2–6 1/2 cups	2 t	1 t	none	4	2–2 1/2 cups
Quinoa	4 1/2–5 1/2 cups	2 t	1 t	none	none	2 1/4–2 3/4 cups

*Volume of mother will vary from week to week. Precision during feedings will help keep the volume consistent, but the bubbles inside the mother will also impact the final volume measurement.

After the batter is mixed, divide it evenly between your two prepared *Pyrex* loaf pans. Flatten the tops of the loaves with a spatula and brush them with melted butter. Put the plastic covers on (cocked ever so slightly to one side so the bread can breathe), set aside in a warm place (70–73°F), and **wait 6–8 hours** or until the dough is level with the top of your loaf pan (rice breads will be down 1/2" to 1" from the top). You can hasten the process by using a proofer set to 85°F. If using a proofer, you won't need to cover the dishes with their covers, but you will need to fill the water tray.

Preheat oven to 425°F. **Bake** loaves on lowest oven rack for **25–30 minutes,** or until bread is nicely browned and internal temperature reaches 200–205°F. **Bake rice breads** on lowest oven rack for **40 minutes** (this will give you a nice, crisp crust) or until internal temperature reaches 200–205°F. Remove from oven and tip loaves out onto a cooling rack (this will keep your crust crisp on all sides).

Proofing Time: 6–8 hours
Bake Time: 25–30 minutes (40 minutes for rice breads)
Makes: Two 9" loaves

Brown Rice

White

Kamut

CROUTONS

If you have leftover bread or just want to add a little crunch to salads, try this recipe for croutons.

Preheat oven to 300°F.

Cut 1/2 loaf of bread into 3/4" cubes (you should have about 6 cups). Add cubes to a large bowl and toss with 2 T olive oil and 1/2 t salt.

Spread cubes onto a baker's sheet in a single layer. Bake for 50–55 minutes, or until crisp. Cool completely and store in an airtight container.

Now that you've mastered making Beginner Batter Bread, how about playing around with different flavors?

Here are some ideas.

Feta & Pesto Bread

1 recipe Batter Bread in your chosen flour (p. 32)
12 ozs feta cheese, crumbled (about 1 1/3 cups)
2/3 cup pesto

Brown Rice

1. Very generously butter your two 2-qt *Pyrex* bakeware dishes (you'll use about 2 T softened butter for each baking dish) and dust with flour; set aside.

2. Make batter. Mix feta into batter. Add about a quarter of the batter to each of your two prepared *Pyrex* bakeware dishes. Carefully spread pesto in a layer, stopping about 1" in from the sides. Evenly divide remaining batter between bakeware dishes, flatten tops of loaves with a spatula, and brush with melted butter.

3. Put the lids on (cocked ever so slightly to one side so the bread can breathe), set aside in a warm place (70–73°F), and wait 6–8 hours or until the dough is level with the top of your bakeware dish (rice breads will be down 1/2" to 1" from the top). You can hasten the process by using a proofer with shelf kit set to 85°F. If using a proofer, you won't need to cover the dishes with their lids, but you will need to fill the water tray.

4. Preheat oven to 425°F. Bake on lowest oven rack for 25–30 minutes, or until bread is nicely browned and internal temperature reaches 200–205°F. Bake rice breads on lowest oven rack for 40 minutes (this will give you a nice, crisp crust) or until internal temperature reaches 200–205°F. Remove from oven and tip loaves out onto a cooling rack (this will keep your crust crisp on all sides).

Einka

White Rice

Einkorn

For All Flavored Batter Breads

Proofing Time:
6–8 hours

Bake Time:
25–30 minutes (40 minutes for rice breads)

Makes:
Two 8 1/2"-round loaves

Asiago, Garlic & Rosemary Bread

1 recipe Batter Bread in your chosen flour (p. 32)
8 ozs Asiago cheese, cut into 1/2" cubes (about 2 cups)
6 garlic cloves, peeled and minced (about 2 T)
3 sprigs fresh rosemary, minced (about 1 1/2 t)

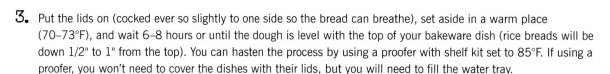

1. Very generously butter your two 2-qt *Pyrex* bakeware dishes (you'll use about 2 T softened butter for each baking dish) and dust with flour; set aside.

2. Make batter. Add Asiago, garlic, and rosemary; mix well. Evenly divide batter between your two prepared *Pyrex* bakeware dishes. Flatten tops of loaves with a spatula and brush with melted butter.

3. Put the lids on (cocked ever so slightly to one side so the bread can breathe), set aside in a warm place (70–73°F), and wait 6–8 hours or until the dough is level with the top of your bakeware dish (rice breads will be down 1/2" to 1" from the top). You can hasten the process by using a proofer with shelf kit set to 85°F. If using a proofer, you won't need to cover the dishes with their lids, but you will need to fill the water tray.

4. Preheat oven to 425°F. Bake loaves on lowest oven rack for 25–30 minutes or until bread is nicely browned and internal temperature reaches 200–205°F. Bake rice breads on lowest oven rack for 40 minutes (this will give you a nice, crisp crust), or until internal temperature reaches 200–205°F. Remove from oven and tip loaves out onto a cooling rack (this will keep your crust crisp on all sides).

Caraway–Dill Bread

1 recipe Batter Bread in your chosen flour (p. 32)
3 T caraway, divided
1/4 cup fresh dill, minced
1 T molasses (optional)

1. Very generously butter your two 2-qt *Pyrex* bakeware dishes (you'll use about 2 T softened butter for each baking dish), and dust with flour; set aside.

2. Make batter. Using a mortar and pestle, lightly crush 1 T caraway. Add all caraway, dill, and molasses (if using) to batter; mix well. Evenly divide batter between your two prepared *Pyrex* bakeware dishes. Flatten tops of loaves with a spatula, and brush with melted butter.

3. Put the lids on (cocked ever so slightly to one side so the bread can breathe), set aside in a warm place (70–73°F), and wait 6–8 hours or until the dough is level with the top of your bakeware dish (rice breads will be down 1/2" to 1" from the top). You can hasten the process by using a proofer with shelf kit set to 85°F. If using a proofer, you won't need to cover the dishes with their lids, but you will need to fill the water tray.

4. Preheat oven to 425°F. Bake loaves on lowest oven rack for 25–30 minutes or until bread is nicely browned and internal temperature reaches 200–205°F. Bake rice breads on lowest oven rack for 40 minutes (this will give you a nice, crisp crust), or until internal temperature reaches 200–205°F. Remove from oven and tip loaves out onto a cooling rack (this will keep your crust crisp on all sides).

Cinnamon-Raisin Bread with Streusel

1 recipe for streusel in your chosen flour, prepared in advance (**see chart below**)
1 recipe Batter Bread in your chosen flour (p. 32)
1 1/4 cups golden raisins
4 t cinnamon
4 t honey

1. Make Streusel in advance to allow time for it to harden in the refrigerator. In a medium bowl, combine flour, brown sugar, walnuts, and melted butter. Line a lidded 2-cup container with wax paper and firmly pack streusel into container. Refrigerate at least 2 hours. Just before making bread, use wax paper to lift streusel from container and cut into 1/2" cubes.

2. Very generously butter your two 2-qt *Pyrex* bakeware dishes (you'll use about 2 T softened butter for each baking dish) and dust with flour; set aside.

3. Make batter. Add streusel, raisins, cinnamon, and honey. Evenly divide batter between your two prepared *Pyrex* bakeware dishes. Flatten tops of loaves with a spatula and brush with melted butter.

4. Put the lids on (cocked ever so slightly to one side so the bread can breathe), set aside in a warm place (70–73°F), and wait 6–8 hours or until the dough is level with the top of your bakeware dish (rice breads will be down 1/2" to 1" from the top). You can hasten the process by using a proofer with shelf kit set to 85°F. If using a proofer, you won't need to cover the dishes with their lids, but you will need to fill the water tray.

5. Preheat oven to 425°F. Bake loaves on lowest oven rack for 25–30 minutes, or until bread is nicely browned and internal temperature reaches 200–205°F. Bake rice breads on lowest oven rack for 40 minutes (this will give you a nice, crisp crust) or until internal temperature reaches 200–205°F. Remove from oven and tip loaves out onto a cooling rack (this will keep your crust crisp on all sides).

Streusel

	Flour (same type as mother)	Brown Sugar	Walnuts (finely chopped)	Butter (melted)
White	3/4 cup	1/2 cup	1/4 cup	5 T
Kamut	3/4 cup	1/2 cup	1/4 cup	4 T
Sprouted	3/4 cup	1/2 cup	1/4 cup	4 T
Einkorn	3/4 cup	1/2 cup	1/4 cup	4 T
Einka	3/4 cup	1/2 cup	1/4 cup	4 T
White Rice	3/4 cup	1/2 cup	1/4 cup	8 T
Brown Rice	3/4 cup	1/2 cup	1/4 cup	5 T
Quinoa	3/4 cup	1/2 cup	1/4 cup	5 T

Cheddar, Corn & Jalapeño Bread

1 recipe Batter Bread in your chosen flour (p. 32)
8 ozs Cheddar cheese, cut into 1/2" cubes (about 2 cups)
1/4 cup corn flour
1/2 jalapeño pepper, seeded and minced (about 1 T)

Kamut

1. Very generously butter your two 2-qt *Pyrex* bakeware dishes (you'll use about 2 T softened butter for each baking dish) and dust with flour; set aside.

2. Make batter. Add Cheddar, corn flour, and jalapeño; mix well. Evenly divide batter between your two prepared *Pyrex* bakeware dishes. Flatten tops of loaves with a spatula and brush with melted butter.

3. Put the lids on (cocked ever so slightly to one side so the bread can breathe), set aside in a warm place (70–73°F), and wait 6–8 hours or until the dough is level with the top of your bakeware dish (rice breads will be down 1/2" to 1" from the top). You can hasten the process by using a proofer with shelf kit set to 85°F. If using a proofer, you won't need to cover the dishes with their lids, but you will need to fill the water tray.

4. Preheat oven to 425°F. Bake loaves on lowest oven rack for 25–30 minutes, or until bread is nicely browned and internal temperature reaches 200–205°F. Bake rice breads on lowest oven rack for 40 minutes (this will give you a nice, crisp crust) or until internal temperature reaches 200–205°F. Remove from oven and tip loaves out onto a cooling rack (this will keep your crust crisp on all sides).

3-Seed Bread

1 recipe Batter Bread in your chosen flour (p. 32)
1/3 cup tri-color quinoa (equal parts golden, red, and black quinoa)
1/4 cup pumpkin seeds, diced
2 T brown flaxseeds

White Rice

1. Very generously butter your two 2-qt *Pyrex* bakeware dishes (you'll use about 2 T softened butter for each baking dish) and dust with flour; set aside.

2. Make batter. Add quinoa, pumpkin seeds, and flaxseeds; mix well. Evenly divide batter between your two prepared *Pyrex* bakeware dishes. Flatten tops of loaves with a spatula and brush with melted butter.

3. Put the lids on (cocked ever so slightly to one side so the bread can breathe), set aside in a warm place (70–73°F), and wait 6–8 hours or until the dough is level with the top of your bakeware dish (rice breads will be down 1/2" to 1" from the top). You can hasten the process by using a proofer with shelf kit set to 85°F. If using a proofer, you won't need to cover the dishes with their lids, but you will need to fill the water tray.

4. Preheat oven to 425°F. Bake loaves on lowest oven rack for 25–30 minutes or until bread is nicely browned and internal temperature reaches 200–205°F. Bake rice breads on lowest oven rack for 40 minutes (this will give you a nice, crisp crust), or until internal temperature reaches 200–205°F. Remove from oven and tip loaves out onto a cooling rack (this will keep your crust crisp on all sides).

3-Grain Bread

1 recipe Batter Bread in your chosen flour (p. 32)
1/2 cup cracked wheat
1/2 cup cracked rye (rye chops)
1/4 cup brown flaxseeds

1. Very generously butter your two 2-qt *Pyrex* bakeware dishes (you'll use about 2 T softened butter for each baking dish) and dust with flour; set aside.

2. Make batter. Add cracked wheat, cracked rye (rye chops), and flaxseeds; mix well. Evenly divide batter between your two prepared *Pyrex* bakeware dishes. Flatten tops of loaves with a spatula and brush with melted butter.

3. Put the lids on (cocked ever so slightly to one side so the bread can breathe), set aside in a warm place (70–73°F), and wait 6–8 hours or until the dough is level with the top of your bakeware dish (rice breads will be down 1/2" to 1" from the top). You can hasten the process by using a proofer with shelf kit set to 85°F. If using a proofer, you won't need to cover the dishes with their lids, but you will need to fill the water tray.

4. Preheat oven to 425°F. Bake loaves on lowest oven rack for 25–30 minutes, or until bread is nicely browned and internal temperature reaches 200–205°F. Remove from oven and tip loaves out onto a cooling rack (this will keep your crust crisp on all sides).

Sprouted

Einkorn

3-GRAIN STORY

Joseph's 3-grain cereal was legendary in its day and the first of its kind. Long before 7-grain and even 12-grain mixes became commonplace commodities in modern-day health-food stores, Joseph was cracking organic wheat and rye on his father's 100-year-old stone mill, adding "a cup or so of flaxseeds," and then stitching the top of each sack shut using white cotton thread. Most of his 3-grain followers were of his generation and happy to trade in their daily hot oatmeal for something more exotic and "healthier."

White Rice

Quinoa

Einkorn

Tip: To brown the surface of white- or brown-rice Dutch-oven loaves (quinoa browns beautifully on its own), dissolve 1/2 t baking soda in 1/4 cup water. Transfer to a spray bottle and mist tops of loaves as recipe directs.

It's the night BEFORE Bake Day. You've been feeding and nurturing your Counter Mother all week, and per the instructions on p. 28, you end up with an 8-cup *Pyrex* "bowl" filled with batter the morning of the seventh day. Instead, the night before, you're going feed your mother her dinner as usual, stir, and then round up a large mixing bowl (at least 4 qt) and put your entire mother* in it. Wash your *Glasslock* bowl and *Marinex* baking dish, remove 1/2 cup mother from your large mixing bowl and return it to your bowl/baking dish setup, and cover. This is now your mother that you'll feed 2x/day until your next Bake Day. Now, before calling it a day, you're going to take the "activated batter" in your large mixing bowl and mix up a stiffer dough with a stronger sourdough flavor that rises 18–20 hours before baking.

Depending on the type of flour you're using, follow the amounts in the chart below.

	Activated Batter	Salt	Water	Flour (same type as mother)
White	6–7 cups	2 t	none	3–3 1/2 cups
Kamut	5 1/2–6 1/2 cups	2 t	none	1 3/4–2 1/4 cups
Sprouted	5 1/2–6 1/2 cups	2 t	none	1 3/4–2 1/4 cups
Einkorn	6–7 cups	2 t	none	4–4 1/2 cups
Einka	5 1/2–6 1/2 cups	2 t	none	4–4 1/2 cups
White Rice	6–7 cups	2 t	1/2 cup	1 1/4–1 3/4 cups
Brown Rice	5 1/2–6 1/2 cups	2 t	none	2 1/4–2 3/4 cups
Quinoa	4 1/2–5 1/2 cups	2 t	none	3 3/4–4 1/4 cups

White

*Volume of mother will vary from week to week. Precision during feedings will help keep the volume consistent, but the bubbles inside the mother will also impact the final volume measurement.

1. To the batter in your bowl, add salt and mix well (if you're making white-rice bread, also note that you'll add water).

2. Start with the smallest amount of your chosen flour in the chart above and add incrementally until you have moist dough that holds its shape. To test this, mound dough up and stop stirring. If it settles quickly, you need to add more flour. After you have the dough all mixed up, cover the bowl with a dinner plate and let rise in a warm place (70–73°F) for 18–20 hours, or until dough is near the top of the bowl.

3. After 18–20 hours, place a 5- to 6-qt lidded cast-iron Dutch oven in the center of oven and preheat to 500°F.

4. Generously dust a clean work surface with flour and scoop dough from bowl. Divide dough into two equal portions and shape into balls, dusting with flour as needed. Cover with a flour-sack cotton towel until oven is preheated.

5. Once oven is preheated, remove Dutch oven and lightly dust with flour. Place one ball of dough into Dutch oven and cover. Bake for 20 minutes; remove lid; spray with baking-soda mixture, if using (see tip at left); and bake an additional 8–10 minutes, or until crust is nicely browned, and internal temperature reaches 200–205°F.

6. Remove loaf from Dutch oven and transfer to a cooling rack. Repeat process with second ball of dough.

Proofing Time: 18–20 hours   Bake Time: 56–60 minutes   Makes: Two 6 1/2" loaves

"I refer to heirloom einkorn and emmer as wild grains. And I use the term whole-grain flour, as opposed to whole-wheat flour, even though both grains are technically wheat."

– Sam Lucy, organic wild-grain farmer, Winthrop, Washington, BluebirdGrainFarms.com

Einkorn

Einkorn Wheat

Einkorn is one of the oldest wheats known to scientists. The term "einkorn" is derived from the German language and interpreted to mean "single grain." Einkorn grows very tall, as wheat did long ago, but **each einkorn kernel is a third of the size of today's wheat.**

It's Bake Day. You've been feeding and nurturing your Counter Mother all week, and per the instructions on p. 28, you're going to put your entire mother into your 8-cup *Pyrex* "bowl," wash your *Glasslock* bowl and *Marinex* baking dish, remove 1/2 cup mother from your "bowl" and return it to your clean bowl/baking dish setup, feed your mother breakfast: 3/8 cup flour and 1/4 cup water, and stir/cover. This is now your mother that you'll feed 2x/day until your next Bake Day. The "activated batter" left in your *Pyrex* "bowl" is now ready to go to work for you.

48

Because this recipe doesn't utilize all of the Counter Mother accumulated in one week, you can use the extra for a double batch of pizza or to make some of the treats in Section 3, Quick & Easy Sourdough-Enhanced Treats, p. 172. Or you can portion the extra into handy 1/2-cup packages and freeze for later use. In this instance, it's okay to freeze portions of your mother because you won't be using it to give rise to bread, but to enhance the flavor and nutritive benefits of quick-and-easy treats like pancakes, waffles, and muffins that use baking powder for loft.

To make pizza, depending on the type of flour you're using, follow the amounts in the chart below.

	Activated Batter	Water	Safflower Oil	Honey	Salt	Semolina Flour	Cornmeal	Flour (same type as mother)
White	2 cups	none	1 T	1 t	1/2 t	1/4 cup	none	1 1/4–1 3/4 cups
Kamut	3 cups	none	1 T	1 t	1/2 t	1/4 cup	none	1–1 1/2 cups
Sprouted	2 cups	none	1 T	1 t	1/2 t	1/4 cup	none	3/4–1 1/4 cups
Einkorn	2 cups	none	1 T	1 t	1/2 t	1/4 cup	none	2–2 1/2 cups
Einka	2 cups	none	1 T	1 t	1/2 t	1/4 cup	none	1 1/2–2 cups
White Rice	3 cups	1/4 cup	1 T	1 t	1/2 t	none	1/4 cup	1/2–3/4 cups
Brown Rice	3 cups	none	1 T	1 t	1/2 t	none	1/4 cup	3/4–1 1/4 cups
Quinoa	3 cups	none	1 T	1 t	1/2 t	none	1/4 cup	1–1 1/2 cups

1. After paring down the amount of batter in your "bowl," add water (if making white-rice crust), safflower oil, honey, salt, and semolina (or cornmeal, if making gluten-free crust).

2. Start with the smallest amount of your chosen flour and add incrementally until dough is smooth and pliable. Lightly dust a clean work surface with flour and scoop dough out of "bowl."

3. Wash and dry "bowl" and coat with safflower oil. Shape dough into a ball and add to "bowl." Cover with plastic wrap and refrigerate until ready to use (up to 12 hours).

4. When you are ready to make pizza, remove dough from refrigerator.

5. Preheat oven to 425°F. Line two 14" pizza pans with parchment paper (if you prefer a slightly thicker crust, use 12" pizza pans).

6. Dust a clean work surface with flour. Scoop dough out of "bowl" and divide dough in half. Roll each half into a 15" circle, dusting with flour as needed, and transfer circles to prepared pizza pans. Shape edges according to preference (for rice crusts, use the back side of a spoon to smooth out crust). Poke a few holes in each crust with a fork to prevent air bubbles and let dough rest, uncovered, for 15 minutes.

7. Bake crusts at the same time for 10 minutes. Remove from oven. Add sauce, cheese, and toppings of your choice.

8. Bake pizzas for 10–15 minutes, rotating pans halfway through, until cheese is melted and bubbling.

9. Remove pizzas from oven. Use a spatula to help slide pizzas to a cooling rack (this keeps crusts crisp). Cut with kitchen shears.

Sprouted

White Rice

Einkorn

Brown Rice

Quinoa

It's Bake Day. You've been feeding and nurturing your Counter Mother all week, and per the instructions on p. 28, you're going to put your entire mother* into your 8-cup *Pyrex* "bowl," wash your *Glasslock* bowl and *Marinex* baking dish, remove 1/2 cup mother from your "bowl" and return it to your clean bowl/baking dish setup, feed your mother breakfast: 3/8 cup flour and 1/4 cup water, and stir/cover. This is now your mother that you'll feed 2x/day until your next Bake Day. The "activated batter" left in your *Pyrex* "bowl" is now ready to be turned into English Muffins.

Depending on the type of flour you're using, follow the amounts in the chart below.

	Activated Batter	Milk	Honey	Salt	Butter (divided)	Corn Flour (divided)	Flour (same type as mother)
White	6–7 cups	1 cup	1/4 cup	1 1/2 t	8 T	4 t	5 3/4–6 1/4 cups
Kamut	5 1/2–6 1/2 cups	1 cup	1/4 cup	1 1/2 t	8 T	4 t	2 1/2–3 cups
Sprouted	5 1/2–6 1/2 cups	1 cup	1/4 cup	1 1/2 t	8 T	4 t	3–3 1/2 cups
Einkorn	6–7 cups	1 cup	1/4 cup	1 1/2 t	8 T	4 t	6–6 1/2 cups
Einka	5 1/2–6 1/2 cups	1 cup	1/4 cup	1 1/2 t	8 T	4 t	5–5 1/2 cups
White Rice	6–7 cups	1 cup	1/4 cup	1 1/2 t	8 T	4 t	2–2 1/2 cups
Brown Rice	5 1/2–6 1/2 cups	1 cup	1/4 cup	1 1/2 t	8 T	4 t	3 1/2–4 cups
Quinoa	4 1/2–5 1/2 cups	1 cup	1/4 cup	1 1/2 t	8 T	4 t	6–6 1/2 cups

*Volume of mother will vary from week to week. Precision during feedings will help keep the volume consistent, but the bubbles inside the mother will also impact the final volume measurement.

1. To the batter in your "bowl," add milk, honey, and salt; mix well. Cover loosely with plastic wrap or a dinner plate and let condition in a warm place (70–73°F) for 2 hours.

2. Melt 2 T butter and brush two baker's sheets with 1 1/2 t each (reserve remaining melted butter for step 4). Sprinkle each baking sheet with 1 t corn flour.

3. Transfer mother from your 8-cup *Pyrex* measuring "bowl" to a large mixing bowl. Start with the smallest amount of your chosen flour in the chart above and add incrementally until dough is smooth, elastic, and shapeable.

4. Generously dust a clean work surface with flour and transfer dough from bowl. Flatten dough to 3/4" thickness. Using a 3" biscuit or cookie cutter, cut dough into rounds. Place rounds on prepared baking sheets, brush tops with remaining melted butter, sprinkle with remaining corn flour, and let rise uncovered on counter for 30 minutes.

5. Preheat oven to 350°F.

6. In a large skillet over low heat, melt 1 T butter. Add English muffins in batches and fry for 1–2 minutes, flip over, and fry an additional 1–2 minutes.

7. After frying, return muffins to prepared baking sheets and fry another batch, adding more butter to pan as needed. Once all muffins are fried, bake in preheated oven for 20–25 minutes, rotating baking sheets halfway through, until muffins are golden and internal temperature reaches 200–205°F.

Proofing Time: 2 hours, 30 minutes
Bake Time: 20–25 minutes **Makes:** Twenty-four to thirty English muffins, depending on type of flour used

Sprouted

Tip: For perfectly golden-brown rolls, brush tops with milk halfway through baking.

White

Quinoa

It's Bake Day. You've been feeding and nurturing your Counter Mother all week, and per the instructions on p. 28, you're going to put your entire mother* into your 8-cup *Pyrex* "bowl," wash your *Glasslock* bowl and *Marinex* baking dish, remove 1/2 cup mother from your "bowl" and return it to your clean bowl/baking dish setup, feed your mother breakfast: 3/8 cup flour and 1/4 cup water, and stir/cover. This is now your mother that you'll feed 2x/day until your next Bake Day. The "activated batter" left in your *Pyrex* "bowl" is now ready to be turned into hot, buttery rolls in time for either lunch or your evening meal.

Depending on the type of flour you're using, follow the amounts in the chart below.

	Activated Batter	Buttermilk	Honey	Salt	Eggs	Flour (same type as mother)
White	6–7 cups	3/4 cup	2 T	1 1/2 t	none	5 1/4–5 3/4 cups
Kamut	5 1/2–6 1/2 cups	3/4 cup	2 T	1 1/2 t	none	3 1/4–3 3/4 cups
Sprouted	5 1/2–6 1/2 cups	3/4 cup	2 T	1 1/2 t	none	3 1/2–4 cups
Einkorn	6–7 cups	3/4 cup	2 T	1 1/2 t	none	6–6 1/2 cups
Einka	5 1/2–6 1/2 cups	3/4 cup	2 T	1 1/2 t	none	5 1/2–6 cups
White Rice	6–7 cups	3/4 cup	2 T	1 1/2 t	2	2 1/2–3 cups
Brown Rice	5 1/2–6 1/2 cups	3/4 cup	2 T	1 1/2 t	2	4 1/4–4 3/4 cups
Quinoa	4 1/2–5 1/2 cups	3/4 cup	2 T	1 1/2 t	2	5 3/4–6 1/4 cups

* Volume of mother will vary from week to week. Precision during feedings will help keep the volume consistent, but the bubbles inside the mother will also impact the final volume measurement.

1. To the batter in your "bowl," add buttermilk, honey, and salt (and eggs, if using); mix well. Cover loosely with plastic wrap or a dinner plate and let condition in a warm place (70–73°F) for 2 hours.

2. Transfer batter from your 8-cup "bowl" to a large mixing bowl (at least 4 qt). Start with the smallest amount of your chosen flour in the chart above and add incrementally until dough is smooth, elastic, and shapeable. Lightly dust a clean work surface with flour and scoop dough out of bowl.

3. Wash and dry large mixing bowl and coat with butter. Shape dough into a ball and add to bowl. Cover with plastic wrap and refrigerate until ready to use (up to 12 hours).

4. When you are ready to make rolls, remove dough from refrigerator.

5. Melt 2 T butter and brush two baker's sheets with 1 T butter each.

6. Divide dough into 24 equal portions. Shape each portion into a ball by pulling and smoothing dough to form the top of the roll in the palm of your hand while pinching the bottom together until the top is smooth. Flip over and place on baking sheets about 2" apart; brush tops with remaining melted butter; and let rise, uncovered, on counter for 45 minutes.

White Rice

7. Preheat oven to 350°F. Bake rolls for 25–30 minutes; rotating baking sheets halfway through, until rolls are light-golden brown and internal temperature reaches 200–205°F.

Einkorn

See Section 5, Equipment, p. 209

It's Bake Day. You've been feeding and nurturing your Counter Mother all week, and per the instructions on p. 28, you're going to put your entire mother* into your 8-cup *Pyrex* "bowl," wash your *Glasslock* bowl and *Marinex* baking dish, remove 1/2 cup mother from your "bowl" and return it to your clean bowl/baking dish setup, feed your mother breakfast: 3/8 cup flour and 1/4 cup water, and stir/cover. This is now your mother that you'll feed 2x/day until your next Bake Day. The "activated batter" left in your *Pyrex* "bowl" is now ready to go to work for you. If you're short on time and can't wait for bread to rise, change it up with these fruit-and-nut-laden crackers (or breakfast/snack bread, if not drying into crackers).

Pick a mixture below, mix fruit and nuts together in a large bowl, and set aside.

Fruit & Nut Options

Dates (pitted and diced)	Dried Apricots (diced)	Golden Raisins	Cashews (chopped)	Blanched Almonds (chopped)	Walnuts (chopped)	Flaxseed (chopped)
18 (about 1 1/2 cups)	1 1/2 cups	1 1/2 cups	1 cup	1 cup	1 cup	1/2 cup

Dates (pitted and diced)	Dried Cranberries	Golden Raisins	Pecans (chopped)	Sunflower Seeds	Pumpkin Seeds (roasted)	Fresh Rosemary
18 (about 1 1/2 cups)	1 1/2 cups	1 1/2 cups	1 cup	1 cup	1 cup	3/4 cup

This recipe makes a lot of batter, so you'll need to transfer it to a large mixing bowl (at least 4 qt).

1. To the batter in your bowl, add honey, safflower oil, baking powder, and salt; stir well. If you're making white-rice bread, also note that you'll add water.

2. Depending on the type of flour you're using and the volume of your mother, you'll need to add varied amounts of flour to reach the desired consistency for baking. Start with the smallest amount of your chosen flour in the chart below and add incrementally until the batter is the consistency of softened cream cheese.

	Activated Batter	Honey	Safflower Oil	Baking Powder	Salt	Water	Flour (same type as mother)
White	6–7 cups	1/3 cup	1/3 cup	2 T	2 t	none	2–2 1/4 cups
Kamut	5 1/2–6 1/2 cups	1/3 cup	1/3 cup	2 T	2 t	none	1/4–1/2 cup
Sprouted	5 1/2–6 1/2 cups	1/3 cup	1/3 cup	2 T	2 t	none	3/4–1 cup
Einkorn	6–7 cups	1/3 cup	1/3 cup	2 T	2 t	none	3–3 1/4 cups
Einka	5 1/2–6 1/2 cups	1/3 cup	1/3 cup	2 T	2 t	none	2 1/4–2 1/2 cups
White Rice	6–7 cups	1/3 cup	1/3 cup	2 T	2 t	1/2 cup	1/2–3/4 cup
Brown Rice	5 1/2–6 1/2 cups	1/3 cup	1/3 cup	2 T	2 t	none	3/4–1 cup
Quinoa	4 1/2–5 1/2 cups	1/3 cup	1/3 cup	2 T	2 t	none	2 1/2–2 3/4 cups

* Volume of mother will vary from week to week. Precision during feedings will help keep the volume consistent, but the bubbles inside the mother will also impact the final volume measurement.

3. Preheat oven to 375°F. Generously butter a lasagna trio pan.

4. Add fruit and nuts and mix well. Divide batter evenly between sections in prepared lasagna pan. Smooth out tops and bake on the center rack in preheated oven for 30–35 minutes, or until internal temperature reaches 200–205°F. Remove from oven and transfer loaves to a cooling rack.

To make into crackers, cool loaves completely and wrap in plastic wrap overnight (this will help soften the crust, making slicing easier).

1. The next day, slice loaves into 1/8"-thick slices. An electric knife or a guillotine bread slicer (right) works well for this.

2. To make dehydrated crackers (makes crackers with a crisp texture and light color): Turn dehydrator to 125–130°F. Arrange slices in a single layer on dehydrator trays. Dry for 8–12 hours, or until crackers are crisp.

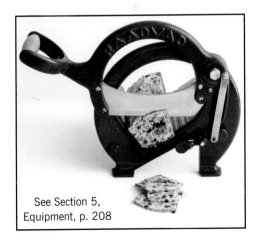

See Section 5, Equipment, p. 208

3. For oven-dried crackers (makes crackers with a crisp texture and deep-golden-brown color): Preheat oven to 225°F. Line two baker's sheets with silicone baking mats or parchment paper. Arrange bread slices in a single layer on prepared baking sheets. Bake for 2 1/2 hours, or until crackers are crisp, rotating baking sheets halfway through.

Bake Time: 30–35 minutes   **Drying Time:** 2 hours, 30 minutes to 12 hours   **Makes:** About ninety crackers

In This Section

*includes gluten-free versions

ADVANCED BREADS

REFRIGERATOR MOTHER

During your time spent establishing and nurturing your mother, for at least a month, you've had a chance to learn the ins and outs of caring for her on a daily basis, and you've baked a variety of delicious breads in the process. In this section, you'll get to take a step back from the daily care of your "Counter Mother" and learn how to maintain her in your refrigerator with weekly feedings and weekly Bake Days.

At this point, your mother should be active, healthy, and lofting breads like in our photos, so go ahead and put her to the test: The morning of Bake Day, take 4 T mother from your *Pyrex* "bowl" and add 2 T to each of two 8-oz jars, gently tapping to help it settle into the bottom of each jar. Place one jar in a warm place that is at least 70–73°F for 3 hours, or in a bread proofer set at 85°F for 2 hours. Place the other jar in the refrigerator. After 3 hours (2 hours, if using a proofer), the mother left in a warm place or proofer should be bubbly and doubled in height, while the mother in the refrigerator should be unchanged. For an easy comparison, set the jar from the refrigerator and the jar left in a warm place or proofer side-by-side. If the mother left in a warm place or proofer is twice as tall as the mother from the refrigerator, she is healthy, active, and ready for more advanced bread making. If the mother left in a warm place or proofer didn't double in height, give her another week of twice-daily feedings and test again.

If your mother does double in height, she's ready to be moved to the refrigerator. The best day to do this is on your chosen Bake Day. This will keep your Bake Day consistent with your Bake Day in the Beginner Section. After you transfer your mother to your 8-cup *Pyrex* "bowl," remove 1/2 cup of mother, and place in the 1.5-qt *Pyrex* loaf pan you used for baking bread in the Beginner Section (p. 38). Feed her 3/8 cup flour and 1/4 cup water (this makes 1 cup of mother). Cover the loaf pan with its lid and place in your refrigerator.

From this point on, your mother will live in your refrigerator. Bake with the mother left in your 8-cup *Pyrex* "bowl" using one of the recipes in the Beginner Section. This will use up your Counter Mother, and you'll be left with only your Refrigerator Mother for Bake Day the following week.

To get your "Refrigerator Mother" ready for Bake Day, she'll spend the night on your kitchen counter with two feedings to liven her up. To get started, you'll need your 10 1/2" *Marinex* baking dish, a flour-sack cotton towel, and your 3.75-qt *Glasslock* bowl. Here's how to prepare your Refrigerator Mother for Bake Day:

1. The night before Bake Day, pour 1/2" purified water into your 10 1/2" *Marinex* baking dish. Place a folded flour-sack cotton towel in the water.

2. Take your mother from the refrigerator and remove 1/2 cup of mother from your 1.5-qt *Pyrex* loaf pan and add it to your *Glasslock* bowl.

3. Feed both the mother in your *Glasslock* bowl and the mother in your 1.5-qt *Pyrex* loaf pan 3/8 cup flour and 1/4 cup water each. Stir the mothers in both the bowl and the loaf pan thoroughly with a spatula. Cover the mother in your loaf pan with its plastic cover and place her back in the refrigerator until next week.

4. Wring the water from your towel back into the baking dish, place your bowl inside the baking dish, and then cover the bowl with the moist towel, tucking the edges down into the water in the baking dish. Let the mother rest on your counter overnight (up to 10 hours).

5. The next morning, **Bake Day**, feed your "activated batter" 3/8 cup flour and 1/4 cup water. Tuck it in and wait 2–3 hours until it begins to bubble.

6. Your "activated batter" is now ready to use. This process will give you approximately 1 1/2 cups of batter. Unless otherwise noted, this is the amount of "activated batter" the recipes in this Advanced Section require.

If you want to take a break from Bake Day,

continue feeding your Refrigerator Mother 3/8 cup flour and 1/4 cup water once a week, for up to 4 weeks. To resume Bake Days, follow the steps outlined above. If you do take a break and then want to start baking again, you can add an extra Bake Day to use up any extra Refrigerator Mother that accumulated during your break from baking, or put it in your freezer in handy 1/2-cup packages to use in one of the recipes in Section 3, Quick & Easy Sourdough-Enhanced Treats, p. 172.

Pardon my French. And also my Greek, Hebrew, Italian, Polish, and Welsh. For this Advanced Section, I wanted to offer some recipes from around the world, because epicurean breads are a daily ritual for billions of people in countries that span the globe. As my DIL and I were perfecting both well-known and little-known international breads into true-blue wild-yeast recipes, I must admit that I felt self-conscious whenever I tried to remember how I was supposed to pronounce some of them. So, I listened to online audios. That only made it worse, because regional accents offered up several different ways to pronounce each one, not to mention that tricky little plural problem on some of the breads when the "s" only shows up in print but is silent when pronounced.

"I'll take a coffee and two of those little crescent-shaped pastries." Spoken in French, the croissant (pronounced kwah-SAHN, singular, no "s" even when asking for two or more) is not only difficult to properly pronounce, I feel a tad silly trying. I've found that my inborn linguistic abilities are seriously lacking whenever I try to manage the proper adenoidal, back-of-the throat emphasis on certain French syllables. That's when it occurred to me to cut myself a little slack by coming up with pronunciations that are not only easy to say and remember, but recognizable to those around me, as if I had walked into a coffee shop in Idaho rather than in France. "I'll take a coffee and two kruh-SAHNTS (with a "t" and an "s"). I decided to offer up pronunciations for the breads in this section that are as easy to speak as French toast (pain perdu). And as easy to remember as coffee with milk (café au lait).

Advanced Equipment ✓ List

These items were already gathered together for the Beginner Section, p. 25:

ONE 3.75-qt *Glasslock* 10 1/2" mixing bowl
ONE 10 1/2" *Marinex* baking dish
TWO 2-qt *Pyrex* bakeware dishes with lids
TWO 1.5-qt *Pyrex* sculpted loaf pans with covers
ONE 8-cup *Pyrex* measuring cup
ONE 5- to 6-qt lidded cast-iron Dutch oven
TWO 13" x 18" baker's sheets
ONE lasagna trio pan
ONE 1/8-cup coffee scoop
TWO silicone spatulas
ONE 12-PACK 28" x 28" flour-sack cotton towels
ONE quick-read digital thermometer
ONE 4-oz spray bottle
ONE *Brød & Taylor* folding bread proofer and yogurt maker with shelf kit (proofer is optional, but highly recommended)*

☐ TWO *Norpro* 8"L x 4.5"W x 3"H nonstick bread pans

☐ ONE *Norpro* 10"L x 4.5"W x 3"H nonstick bread pan
-OR-
ONE *Jamie Oliver* 1.5-liter 8"L x 5"W x 4"H nonstick loaf tin

☐ ONE *USA Pan* 13"L x 4"W x 4"H nonstick Pullman loaf pan

☑ FOUR mini loaf pans 5"L x 3.25"W x 2.25"H

☐ ONE oval baking tin 15.75"L x 4"W x 2.75"H (for gluten-free French bread)

☑ ONE 13"L x 9"W x 2.5"H glass baking dish

☑ ONE enameled cast-iron Dutch oven or enameled cast-iron skillet at least 7" in diameter

☑ ONE 12" cast-iron skillet

☑ ONE 15"-square pizza stone

☑ ONE pizza peel

☐ ONE baker's linen

☐ ONE baguette board

☑ ONE bread lame

☑ ONE 8"-round banneton proofing basket

☐ ONE wooden dough scraper

☑ ONE bowl scraper

☐ ONE 6" stainless-steel skimmer

☑ FIFTY baking parchment paper half-sheets**

Resources
*BrodAndTaylor.com
**KingArthurFlour.com

The fine print ...

This is a list of frequently (and not-so-frequently) used equipment throughout this section. This list, along with basic kitchen equipment (and a few specialty, non-essential items like a bread machine), will get you through the recipes in this section. For a more detailed, itemized discussion, see Section 5, Equipment, p. 200. We suggest looking through the advanced recipes to decide, for instance, if you'll be making loaves of boule, and if so, whether or not you need to purchase a banneton basket. We also give make-do tips in Section 5 for using substitutes like a bowl lined with a flour-sack cotton towel when making boule. Of course, we think you'll want to make each and every bread we've featured. If you're already making bread, much of what is on this list is probably already in your kitchen.

Items listed are commonly available online (simply use the specific name we've provided for an online search) or check with your local kitchen store.

(bah TARD)

plural: bâtards (same pronunciation; silent "s")

The French bread family consists of breads that have the same basic ingredients but varied proofing and shaping techniques. Perhaps the most famous bread in this family is the baguette. A baguette typically weighs 8 ozs and is 24" in length, which is too long for most domestic ovens. A lesser-known relative of the baguette is the bâtard. Bâtards are the same width, but shorter than a baguette, 12"–16" in length, making them suitable for baking in domestic ovens. Bâtards have a thin, crisp exterior and a soft, yet substantial, interior with sporadic, medium-sized holes.

Einkorn

Tip: Why do I need to invert my baking sheet? Inverting the baking sheet adds support to larger loaves of breads and streamlines transferring loaves to the pizza peel and oven because you don't have the baking-sheet rims to contend with.

It's the night BEFORE Bake Day (p. 58). As usual, you're going to pull 1/2 cup mother from your Refrigerator Mother, feed her 3/8 cup flour and 1/4 cup water, stir/cover, and put her back until next week.

To the 1/2 cup mother now in your *Glasslock* bowl that's about to become "activated batter," you'll add 3/8 cup flour and 1/4 cup water; stir/cover.

It's Bake Day. Rise and shine! Feed your activated batter 3/8 cup flour and 1/4 cup water; stir/cover. Two to three hours later, it's ready to go to work for you.

Depending on the type of flour you're using, follow the amounts in the chart below.

	Activated Batter	Water	Salt	Flour (same type as mother)	Ice Cubes	Egg Whites	Sea–Salt Flakes
White	1 1/2 cups	1 cup	1 1/2 t	2 3/4–3 1/4 cups	1 cup	1	1 t
Kamut	1 1/2 cups	1 cup	1 1/2 t	2 1/4–2 3/4 cups	1 cup	1	1 t
Sprouted	1 1/2 cups	1 cup	1 1/2 t	2 1/2–3 cups	1 cup	1	1 t
Einkorn	1 1/2 cups	1 cup	1 1/2 t	4 3/4–5 1/4 cups	1 cup	1	1 t
Einka	1 1/2 cups	1 cup	1 1/2 t	4–4 1/2 cups	1 cup	1	1 t

1. To the batter in your bowl, add water and salt; mix well. Starting with the smallest amount of flour in the chart, reserve 1 cup of it for kneading and add the rest of it to the bowl with the batter; mix until a stiff, tacky dough forms. Let rest 5 minutes.

2. Dust a clean work surface with reserved flour and scoop dough out of bowl. As you begin to work in the reserved flour, resist the urge to add more flour, as it will produce a dense loaf. Instead, very lightly coat your hands with cooking oil to prevent dough from sticking to your hands. If dough is still too sticky after reserved flour has been worked in, begin working in another 1/2 cup of flour. Continue to knead until dough is smooth, pliable, and slightly tacky (about 8 minutes).

(continued on p. 64)

(continued from p. 63)

3. Wash and dry bowl and coat with safflower oil. Shape dough into a ball and add to bowl. Cover bowl with its lid and let rest in a warm place (70–73°F) for 30 minutes.

4. After 30 minutes, remove lid. Starting at the edge of the bowl, lift a portion of the dough toward the center of the bowl using a bowl scraper. Rotate the bowl, lift another portion, and fold it toward the center. Repeat until all edges have been folded toward the center (6–8 total folds). Cover bowl with lid and let rest again in a warm place (70–73°F) for 30 minutes. Repeat fold/rest two more times. Now, you're done with the folding process that conditions the dough so it rises well (step 6).

5. After the last 30 minutes, lightly dust a clean work surface with flour and scoop dough from bowl using the bowl scraper. Divide dough into 3 equal portions and stretch each portion into a 4" x 16" rectangle. Starting from the 16" edge, roll the dough into a rope and pinch the bottom seam closed. Tuck ends of the rope under to create a uniform rope; pinch seams to seal.

6. Generously dust a baker's linen with flour. Roll a single rope onto baguette board and transfer to baker's linen, seam side facing down. Straighten rope on linen and lift the sides of the linen so they cradle the rope. Repeat this process with remaining portions of dough. Cover bâtards with a flour-sack cotton towel and let rise for 45 minutes.

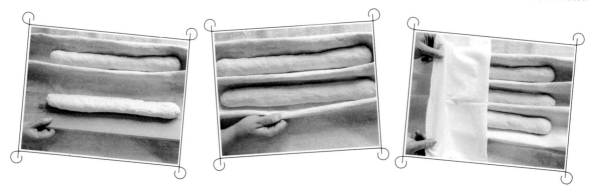

7. Before bread finishes its 45-minute rise, move an oven rack to the center of the oven and another to the bottom. Place an enameled cast-iron Dutch oven on the bottom rack and a 15"-square baking stone on the center rack. Preheat oven to 425°F.

8. Line an inverted baker's sheet with parchment paper. Using baguette board, transfer bâtards from linen to parchment, seam side facing down. Using a bread lame, make swift, superficial, diagonal slashes across bâtards.

9. Slide pizza peel under parchment paper and loaves. Slide loaves and parchment paper off pizza peel onto baking stone. Add ice cubes to enameled cast-iron Dutch oven. (Why? See p. 216.) Bake for 10 minutes.

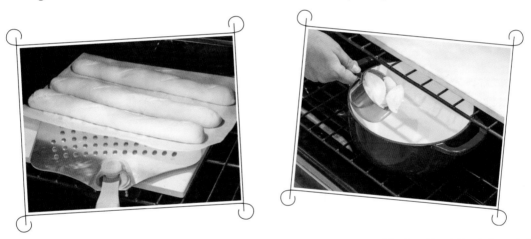

10. Meanwhile, in a small bowl, combine egg white and 1 t water and mix until frothy. After bâtards have baked 10 minutes, remove from oven, using the pizza peel. Brush with egg-white wash and sprinkle with sea-salt flakes. Return to oven and bake an additional 15 minutes or until internal temperature reaches 190°F. Remove from oven and transfer to a cooling rack.

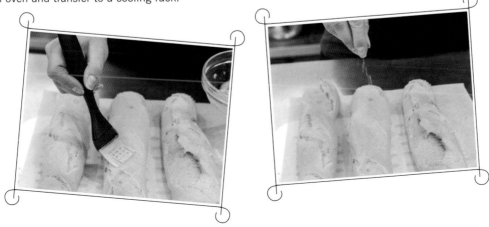

Proofing Time: 2 hours, 45 minutes   Bake Time: 25 minutes   Makes: Three 15" bâtards

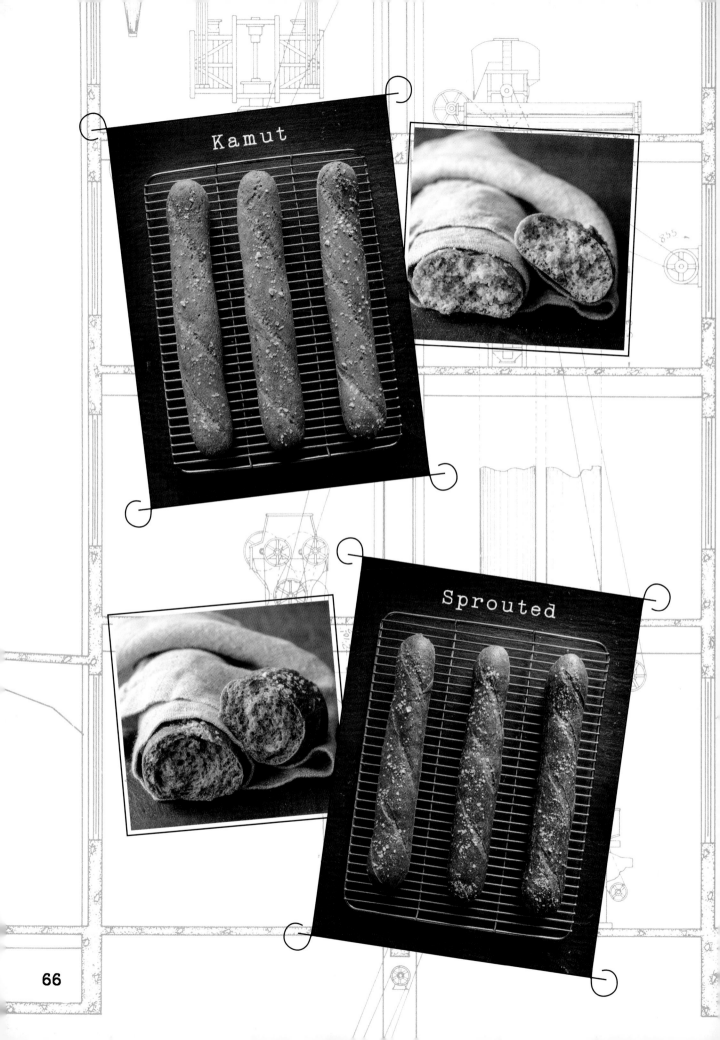

Kamut

Sprouted

Einka

White

White Rice

Brown Rice

It's the night BEFORE Bake Day (p. 58).

As usual, you're going to pull 1/2 cup mother from your Refrigerator Mother, feed her 3/8 cup flour and 1/4 cup water, stir/cover, and put her back until next week.

To the 1/2 cup mother now in your *Glasslock* bowl that's about to become "activated batter," you'll add 3/8 cup flour and 1/4 cup water; stir/cover.

It's Bake Day. Rise and shine! Feed your activated batter 3/8 cup flour and 1/4 cup water; stir/cover. Two to three hours later, it's ready to go to work for you.

Depending on the type of flour you're using, follow the amounts in the chart below.

	Activated Batter	Water	Salt	Flour (same type as mother)	B.F.M. Rice Starch*	Ice Cubes	Egg Whites	Sea-Salt Flakes
White Rice	1 1/2 cups	1 1/2 cups	1 1/2 t	2 cups	1/2 cup	1 cup	1	1 t
Brown Rice	1 1/2 cups	1 1/2 cups	1 1/2 t	3 1/2 cups	3/4 cup	1 cup	1	1 t
Quinoa	1 1/2 cups	1 1/2 cups	1 1/2 t	5 cups	none	1 cup	1	1 t

*Barron Flour Mill rice starch, p. 195

1. To the batter in your bowl, add water and salt; mix well.

2. Add about half the required flour (and the rice starch, if using). Mix until a tacky dough forms; let rest 5 minutes.

3. Mix in remaining flour (dough may seem dry, but it will moisten and come together during conditioning).

4. Cover bowl with its lid and let rest in a warm place (70–73°F) for 30 minutes.

5. After 30 minutes, remove lid. Starting at the edge of the bowl, lift a portion of the dough toward the center of the bowl using a bowl scraper. Rotate the bowl, lift another portion, and fold it toward the center. Repeat until all edges have been folded toward the center (6–8 total folds). Cover bowl with lid and let rest again in a warm place (70–73°F) for 30 minutes. Repeat fold/rest two more times. Now, you're done with the folding process that conditions the dough so it rises well (step 7).

6. After the last 30 minutes, lightly dust a clean work surface with flour and scoop dough from bowl using the bowl scraper. Divide dough into 3 equal portions and roll each portion into a 15" rope, smoothing out imperfections as you work.

7. Generously dust a baker's linen with flour. Roll a single rope onto baguette board and transfer to baker's linen. Straighten rope on linen and lift the sides of the linen so they cradle the rope. Repeat this process with remaining ropes. Cover bâtards with a flour-sack cotton towel and let rise for 45 minutes.

8. Before bread finishes its 45-minute rise, move an oven rack to the center of the oven and another to the bottom. Place an enameled cast-iron Dutch oven on the bottom rack and a 15"-square baking stone on the center rack. Preheat oven to 425°F.

9. Line an inverted baker's sheet with parchment paper. Using a baguette board, transfer bâtards from linen to parchment and spray with baking-soda mixture, if using (see tip at left). Using a bread lame, make swift, superficial, diagonal slashes down bâtards.

10. Slide pizza peel under parchment paper and loaf. Slide bread and parchment paper off pizza peel onto baking stone. Add ice cubes to enameled cast-iron Dutch oven. (Why? See p. 216.) Bake for 10 minutes.

11. Meanwhile, in a small bowl, combine egg white and 1 t water and mix until frothy. After bâtards have baked 10 minutes, remove from oven, using the pizza peel. Brush with egg-white wash and sprinkle with sea-salt flakes. Return to oven and bake an additional 15 minutes or until internal temperature reaches 190°F. Remove from oven and transfer to a cooling rack.

before conditioning

after conditioning

Quinoa

Proofing Time: 2 hours, 45 minutes   Bake Time: 25 minutes   Makes: Three 15" bâtards

BOULE

Boule is a loaf shaped by hand and proofed in a basket (see Section 5, Equipment, p. 206). Resembling a flattened ball once it's baked, the interior texture lands somewhere between a bâtard and French bread, but with fewer holes. Meaning "ball" in French, it's also the reason a bread baker is referred to as a "boulanger" and a bread bakery is called a "boulangerie."

(bOOl—rhymes with cool)
plural: boules (same pronunciation; silent "s")

Kamut

To be on the safe side when pronouncing this bread (bOOl), keep it one syllable, but when spoken in French, the "E" at the end is sort of there, but barely. Actually, the "E" isn't really an "E" but a lingering "L" sound, BOOLlluh. French love consonants, so they hang onto them, letting them go reluctantly (Monet being a clear exception to that boule, I mean rule).

It's the night BEFORE Bake Day (p. 58). As usual, you're going to pull 1/2 cup mother from your Refrigerator Mother, feed her 3/8 cup flour and 1/4 cup water, stir/cover, and put her back until next week.

To the 1/2 cup mother now in your *Glasslock* bowl that's about to become "activated batter," you'll add 3/8 cup flour and 1/4 cup water; stir/cover.

It's Bake Day. Rise and shine! Feed your activated batter 3/8 cup flour and 1/4 cup water; stir/cover. Two to three hours later, it's ready to go to work for you.

Depending on the type of flour you're using, follow the amounts in the chart below.

	Activated Batter	Water	Salt	Flour (same type as mother)	Ice Cubes
White	1 1/2 cups	1 cup	1 1/2 t	2 3/4–3 1/4 cups	1 cup
Kamut	1 1/2 cups	1 cup	1 1/2 t	2 1/4–2 3/4 cups	1 cup
Sprouted	1 1/2 cups	1 cup	1 1/2 t	2 1/2–3 cups	1 cup
Einkorn	1 1/2 cups	3/4 cup	1 1/2 t	4 1/4–4 3/4 cups	1 cup
Einka	1 1/2 cups	1 cup	1 1/2 t	4–4 1/2 cups	1 cup

1. To the batter in your bowl, add water and salt; mix well. Starting with the smallest amount of flour in the chart, reserve 1 cup of it for kneading and add the rest of it to the bowl with the batter; mix until a stiff, tacky dough forms. Let rest 5 minutes.

2. Dust a clean work surface with reserved flour and scoop dough out of bowl. As you begin to work in the reserved flour, resist the urge to add more flour, as it will produce a dense loaf. Instead, very lightly coat your hands with cooking oil to prevent dough from sticking to your hands. If dough is still too sticky after reserved flour has been worked in, begin working in another 1/2 cup of flour. Continue to knead until dough is smooth, pliable, and slightly tacky (about 8 minutes).

3. Wash and dry bowl and coat with safflower oil. Shape dough into a ball and add to bowl. Cover bowl its with lid and let rest in a warm place (70–73°F) for 30 minutes.

4. After 30 minutes, remove lid. Starting at the edge of the bowl, lift a portion of the dough toward the center of the bowl using a bowl scraper. Rotate the bowl, lift another portion, and fold it toward the center. Repeat until all edges have been folded toward the center (6–8 total folds). Cover bowl with lid and let rest again in a warm place (70–73°F) for 30 minutes. Repeat fold/rest two more times. Now, you're done with the folding process that conditions the dough so it rises well (step 6).

5. After the last 30 minutes, generously dust an 8"-round banneton proofing basket with flour; set aside.

6. Lightly dust a clean work surface with flour. Scoop dough from bowl using the bowl scraper. Shape dough into a large ball, pinching seams together at the bottom of the ball. Place in floured banneton basket, seam side facing up. Cover with a flour-sack cotton towel and let rise for 45 minutes.

7. Before bread finishes its 45-minute rise, move an oven rack to the center of the oven and another to the bottom. Place an enameled cast-iron Dutch oven on the bottom rack and a 15"-square baking stone on the center rack. Preheat oven to 425°F.

8. Remove flour-sack cotton towel and place a sheet of parchment paper over loaf. Place pizza peel over parchment paper and flip pizza peel, parchment paper, and banneton basket over. Gently lift banneton basket away from dough.

9. Using a bread lame, make swift, superficial cuts along curves of loaf.

10. Slide bread and parchment paper off pizza peel onto baking stone. Add 1 cup ice cubes to enameled cast-iron Dutch oven. (Why? See p. 216.)

11. Bake for 30–35 minutes, or until internal temperature reaches 190°F. Remove from oven and transfer to a cooling rack.

Proofing Time: 2 hours, 45 minutes   Bake Time: 30–35 minutes   Makes: One 8" boule

Einkorn

To make a quick-and-easy Tomato Garnish, cut two medium tomatoes in half (we like to use one red and one yellow tomato), scoop out the seeds, and discard. Dice the remaining outer tomato flesh and add to a medium bowl. Add 1/4 cup peeled and diced red onion, thinly sliced fresh basil, 1 T balsamic vinegar, 2 t olive oil, 1/2 t honey or grape must, and salt and pepper to taste.

Einkorn

White

Sprouted

FLOUR DRESSER

...EAS MFG. CO. MOLINE, ILL.

Einka

73

Quinoa

Tip: To brown the surface of white- or brown-rice boule (quinoa browns beautifully on its own), dissolve 1/2 t baking soda in 1/4 cup water. Transfer to a spray bottle and mist top of boule before baking.

Brown Rice

White Rice

It's the night BEFORE Bake Day (p. 58). As usual, you're going to pull 1/2 cup mother from your Refrigerator Mother, feed her 3/8 cup flour and 1/4 cup water, stir/cover, and put her back until next week.

To the 1/2 cup mother now in your *Glasslock* bowl that's about to become "activated batter," you'll add 3/8 cup flour and 1/4 cup water; stir/cover.

It's Bake Day. Rise and shine! Feed your activated batter 3/8 cup flour and 1/4 cup water; stir/cover. Two to three hours later, it's ready to go to work for you.

Depending on the type of flour you're using, follow the amounts in the chart below.

	Activated Batter	Water	Salt	Flour (same type as mother)	B.F.M. Rice Starch*	Ice Cubes
White Rice	1 1/2 cups	1 1/2 cups	1 1/2 t	2 cups	1/2 cup	1 cup
Brown Rice	1 1/2 cups	1 1/2 cups	1 1/2 t	3 1/2 cups	3/4 cup	1 cup
Quinoa	1 1/2 cups	1 1/2 cups	1 1/2 t	5 cups	none	1 cup

*Barron Flour Mill rice starch, p. 195

1. To the batter in your bowl, add water and salt; mix well.

2. Add about half the required flour (and the rice starch, if using). Mix until a tacky dough forms; let rest 5 minutes.

3. Mix in remaining flour (dough may seem dry, but it will moisten and come together during conditioning).

4. Cover bowl with its lid and let rest in a warm place (70–73°F) for 30 minutes.

5. After 30 minutes, remove lid. Starting at the edge of the bowl, lift a portion of the dough toward the center of the bowl using a bowl scraper. Rotate the bowl, lift another portion, and fold it toward the center. Repeat until all edges have been folded toward the center (6–8 total folds). Cover bowl with lid and let rest again in a warm place (70–73°F) for 30 minutes. Repeat fold/rest two more times. Now, you're done with the folding process that conditions the dough so it rises well (step 7).

6. After the last 30 minutes, generously dust an 8"-round banneton proofing basket with flour; set aside.

7. Lightly dust a clean work surface with flour. Scoop dough from bowl using the bowl scraper. Shape dough into a large ball, pinching seams together at the bottom of the ball. Place in floured banneton basket, seam side facing up. Cover with a flour-sack cotton towel and let rise for 45 minutes.

8. Before bread finishes its 45-minute rise, move an oven rack to the center of the oven and another to the bottom. Place an enameled cast-iron Dutch oven on the bottom rack and a 15"-square baking stone on the center rack. Preheat oven to 425°F.

9. Remove flour-sack cotton towel and place a sheet of parchment paper over loaf. Place pizza peel over parchment paper and flip pizza peel, parchment paper, and banneton basket over. Gently lift banneton basket away from dough.

10. Using a bread lame, make swift, superficial cuts along curves of loaf. Spray with baking-soda mixture, if using (see tip at left).

11. Slide bread and parchment paper off pizza peel onto baking stone. Add ice cubes to enameled cast-iron Dutch oven. (Why? See p. 216.)

12. Bake for 40–45 minutes, or until internal temperature reaches 190°F. Remove from oven and transfer to a cooling rack.

Remember, a baguette is at least 24" in length. A bâtard is the same width, only shorter, 12"–16" inches in length. And just to make things more interesting, there's also a *ficelle* (FEE say la), p. 86, which means "string" in French. A ficelle is long like a baguette, but more dense, skinnier, and about half the weight. It's like a long breadstick with a lot more crust. (Our version is short, like a bâtard.) What we commonly refer to as French bread is wider than a baguette or bâtard, and certainly wider than a ficelle. A loaf of French bread is the same length as a bâtard, but wider and more oval. It has a thin, crisp crust like all the others, but the holes throughout the loaf are larger. There you have it: papa baguette, mama bâtard, baby ficelle, and stout cousin French with bigger eyes.

White

Tip: What's the secret to soft, lofty bread? Don't add too much flour as you knead it. When you first begin to knead dough, it's going to stick to your counter. But if you resist the urge to add flour every time it starts sticking, you'll discover that "worked" dough starts to absorb its water and bind together better, and eventually, the dough itself will pick up what's stuck to your counter and welcome it back into the fold, literally.

It's the night BEFORE Bake Day (p. 58). As usual, you're going to pull 1/2 cup mother
from your Refrigerator Mother, feed her 3/8 cup flour and 1/4 cup water, stir/cover, and put her back until next week.

To the 1/2 cup mother now in your *Glasslock* bowl that's about to become "activated batter," you'll add 3/8 cup flour and 1/4 cup water; stir/cover.

It's Bake Day. Rise and shine! Feed your activated batter 3/8 cup flour and 1/4 cup water; stir/cover.
Two to three hours later, it's ready to go to work for you.

Depending on the type of flour you're using, follow the amounts in the chart below.

	Activated Batter	Water	Salt	Flour (same type as mother)	Egg Whites	Ice Cubes
White	1 1/2 cups	1 cup	1 1/2 t	2 3/4–3 1/4 cups	1	1 cup
Kamut	1 1/2 cups	1 cup	1 1/2 t	2 1/4–2 3/4 cups	1	1 cup
Sprouted	1 1/2 cups	1 cup	1 1/2 t	2 1/2–3 cups	1	1 cup
Einkorn	1 1/2 cups	1 cup	1 1/2 t	4 3/4–5 1/4 cups	1	1 cup
Einka	1 1/2 cups	1 cup	1 1/2 t	4–4 1/2 cups	1	1 cup

1. To the batter in your bowl, add water and salt; mix well. Starting with the smallest amount of flour in the chart, reserve 1 cup of it for kneading and add the rest of it to the bowl with the batter; mix until a stiff, tacky dough forms. Let rest 5 minutes.

2. Dust a clean work surface with reserved flour and scoop dough out of bowl. As you begin to work in the reserved flour, resist the urge to add more flour, as it will produce a dense loaf. Instead, very lightly coat your hands with cooking oil to prevent dough from sticking to your hands. If dough is still too sticky after reserved flour has been worked in, begin working in another 1/2 cup of flour. Continue to knead until dough is smooth, pliable, and slightly tacky (about 8 minutes).

3. Wash and dry bowl and coat with safflower oil. Shape dough into a ball and add to bowl. Cover bowl with its lid and let rest in a warm place (70–73°F) for 30 minutes.

4. After 30 minutes, remove lid. Starting at the edge of the bowl, lift a portion of the dough toward the center of the bowl using a bowl scraper. Rotate the bowl, lift another portion, and fold it toward the center. Repeat until all edges have been folded toward the center (6–8 total folds). Cover bowl with lid and let rest again in a warm place (70–73°F) for 30 minutes. Repeat fold/rest two more times. Now, you're done with the folding process that conditions the dough so it rises well (step 7).

5. After the last 30 minutes, place a sheet of parchment paper on an inverted baker's sheet; set aside.

6. Lightly dust a clean work surface with flour. Scoop dough from bowl using the bowl scraper. Gently flatten dough into a 10" x 16" rectangle. Starting from the 16" edge, fold the ends about 1/2" in on each side and roll the dough up into a loaf. Pinch the bottom seam closed.

7. Transfer loaf to prepared baking sheet, seam side facing down, cover with a flour-sack cotton towel, and let rise for 45 minutes.

8. Before bread finishes its 45-minute rise, move an oven rack to the center of the oven and another to the bottom. Place an enameled cast-iron Dutch oven on the bottom rack and a 15"-square baking stone on the center rack. Preheat oven to 425°F.

9. In a small bowl, combine egg white and 1 t water and mix until frothy; set aside.

10. Using a bread lame, make swift, superficial, diagonal slashes across loaf. Brush loaf with egg-white wash.

11. Slide pizza peel under parchment paper and loaf. Slide bread and parchment paper off pizza peel onto baking stone. Add 1 cup ice cubes to enameled cast-iron Dutch oven. (Why? See p. 216.)

12. Bake for 25–30 minutes, or until internal temperature reaches 190°F. Remove from oven and transfer to a cooling rack.

Proofing Time: 2 hours, 45 minutes   Bake Time: 25–30 minutes   Makes: One 15" French loaf

Einkorn

Sprouted

GLUTEN-FREE FRENCH BREAD

We prefer baking gluten-free French bread in oval baking tins (see Section 5, Equipment, p. 204) because the loaves have a tendency to flatten as they bake.

Quinoa

Brown Rice

White Rice

Tip: To brown the surface of white- or brown-rice French bread (quinoa browns beautifully on its own), dissolve 1/2 t baking soda in 1/4 cup water. Transfer to a spray bottle and mist tops of loaves before baking.

It's the night BEFORE Bake Day (p. 58). As usual, you're going to pull 1/2 cup mother from your Refrigerator Mother, feed her 3/8 cup flour and 1/4 cup water, stir/cover, and put her back until next week.

To the 1/2 cup mother now in your *Glasslock* bowl that's about to become "activated batter," you'll add 3/8 cup flour and 1/4 cup water; stir/cover.

It's Bake Day. Rise and shine! Feed your activated batter 3/8 cup flour and 1/4 cup water; stir/cover. Two to three hours later, it's ready to go to work for you.

Depending on the type of flour you're using, follow the amounts in the chart below.

	Activated Batter	Water	Salt	Flour (same type as mother)	B.F.M. Rice Starch*	Ice Cubes
White Rice	1 1/2 cups	1 1/2 cups	1 1/2 t	2 cups	1/2 cup	1 cup
Brown Rice	1 1/2 cups	1 1/2 cups	1 1/2 t	3 1/2 cups	3/4 cup	1 cup
Quinoa	1 1/2 cups	1 1/2 cups	1 1/2 t	5 cups	none	1 cup

*Barron Flour Mill rice starch, p. 195

1. To the batter in your bowl, add water and salt; mix well.

2. Add about half the required flour (and the rice starch, if using). Mix until a tacky dough forms; let rest 5 minutes.

3. Mix in remaining flour (dough may seem dry, but it will moisten and come together during conditioning).

4. Cover bowl with its lid and let rest in a warm place (70–73°F) for 30 minutes.

5. After 30 minutes, remove lid. Starting at the edge of the bowl, lift a portion of the dough toward the center of the bowl using a bowl scraper. Rotate the bowl, lift another portion, and fold it toward the center. Repeat until all edges have been folded toward the center (6–8 total folds). Cover bowl with lid and let rest again in a warm place (70–73°F) for 30 minutes. Repeat fold/rest two more times. Now, you're done with the folding process that conditions the dough so it rises well (step 7).

6. After the last 30 minutes, line an inverted baker's sheet with parchment paper. Adjust an oval baking tin to 14" in length. Line inside of tin with parchment paper. (Gluten-free breads don't hold their French-bread shape as well as gluten breads.)

7. Spoon dough into parchment-lined tin and smooth out top. Cover with a flour-sack cotton towel and let rise for 45 minutes.

8. Before bread finishes its 45-minute rise, move an oven rack to the center of the oven and another to the bottom. Place an enameled cast-iron Dutch oven on the bottom rack and a 15"-square baking stone on the center rack. Preheat oven to 425°F.

9. Just before baking, spray loaf with baking-soda mixture, if using (see tip at left). Using a bread lame, make swift, superficial, diagonal slashes down loaf.

10. Slide pizza peel under parchment paper and loaf. Slide bread and parchment paper off pizza peel onto baking stone. Add ice cubes to enameled cast-iron Dutch oven. (Why? See p. 216.)

11. Bake for 15 minutes. Remove from oven using the pizza peel. Remove oval baking tin from loaf. Return loaf to oven and bake an additional 15–20 minutes, or until internal temperature reaches 190°F. Remove from oven and transfer to a cooling rack.

EPI

(a PEA)

plural: epis (same pronunciation; silent "s")

Epi, or pain d'epi, is a French pull-apart bread that mimics a stalk of wheat. It's a perfect pass-around bread when served with soup or a dipping sauce or packed into a picnic basket with a wedge of cheese. And because it has so many cuts and angles that turn crisp in the oven, epi is a favorite among crust lovers.

White

Kamut

Sprouted   Einkorn   Einka

It's the night BEFORE Bake Day (p. 58). As usual, you're going to pull 1/2 cup mother from your Refrigerator Mother, feed her 3/8 cup flour and 1/4 cup water, stir/cover, and put her back until next week.

To the 1/2 cup mother now in your *Glasslock* bowl that's about to become "activated batter," you'll add 3/8 cup flour and 1/4 cup water; stir/cover.

It's Bake Day. Rise and shine! Feed your activated batter 3/8 cup flour and 1/4 cup water; stir/cover. Two to three hours later, it's ready to go to work for you.

Depending on the type of flour you're using, follow the amounts in the chart below.

	Activated Batter	Water	Salt	Flour (same type as mother)	Ice Cubes
White	1 1/2 cups	1 cup	1 1/2 t	2 3/4–3 1/4 cups	1 cup
Kamut	1 1/2 cups	1 cup	1 1/2 t	2 1/4–2 3/4 cups	1 cup
Sprouted	1 1/2 cups	1 cup	1 1/2 t	2 1/2–3 cups	1 cup
Einkorn	1 1/2 cups	1 cup	1 1/2 t	4 3/4–5 1/4 cups	1 cup
Einka	1 1/2 cups	1 cup	1 1/2 t	4–4 1/2 cups	1 cup

1. To the batter in your bowl, add water and salt; mix well. Starting with the smallest amount of flour in the chart, reserve 1 cup of it for kneading and add the rest of it to the bowl with the batter; mix until a stiff, tacky dough forms. Let rest 5 minutes.

2. Dust a clean work surface with reserved flour and scoop dough out of bowl. As you begin to work in the reserved flour, resist the urge to add more flour, as it will produce a dense loaf. Instead, very lightly coat your hands with cooking oil to prevent dough from sticking to your hands. If dough is still too sticky after reserved flour has been worked in, begin working in another 1/2 cup of flour. Continue to knead until dough is smooth, pliable, and slightly tacky (about 8 minutes).

3. Wash and dry bowl and coat with safflower oil. Shape dough into a ball and add to bowl. Cover bowl with its lid and let rest in a warm place (70–73°F) for 30 minutes.

4. After 30 minutes, remove lid. Starting at the edge of the bowl, lift a portion of the dough toward the center of the bowl using a bowl scraper. Rotate the bowl, lift another portion, and fold it toward the center. Repeat until all edges have been folded toward the center (6–8 total folds). Cover bowl with lid and let rest again in a warm place (70–73°F) for 30 minutes. Repeat fold/rest two more times. Now, you're done with the folding process that conditions the dough so it rises well (step 8).

5. After the last 30 minutes, lightly dust a clean work surface with flour and scoop dough from bowl using the bowl scraper. Divide dough into 3 equal portions and stretch each portion into a 4" x 16" rectangle. Starting from the 16" edge, roll the dough into a rope and pinch the bottom seam closed. Tuck ends of the rope under to create a uniform rope; pinch seams to seal.

6–8. (facing page)

9. Before bread finishes its 45-minute rise, move an oven rack to the center of the oven and another to the bottom. Place an enameled cast-iron Dutch oven on the bottom rack. Preheat oven to 425°F.

10. Put epi loaves into oven. Add ice cubes to enameled cast-iron Dutch oven. (Why? See p. 216.)

11. Bake for 25 minutes, or until internal temperature reaches 190°F. Remove from oven and transfer to a cooling rack.

Proofing Time: 2 hours, 45 minutes   Bake Time: 25 minutes   Makes: Three 15" epis

6.
Line an inverted baker's sheet with parchment paper. Roll a single rope onto a baguette board and transfer to prepared baking sheet, seam side facing down. Straighten rope on baking sheet. Repeat this process with remaining portions of dough.

7.
Using kitchen shears, make a 45° angled cut at the top of a rope, leaving the back of the rope intact (about 1/2" up from the bottom). Turn cut piece to the left and make another 45° cut, but this time, turn cut piece to the right.

8.
Continue making cuts and turning cut pieces in alternating directions. Once all ropes have been cut, cover epi loaves with a flour-sack cotton towel and let rise for 45 minutes.

Ficelle (French for "string") is a small, thin loaf of bread that is mostly crust, similar to a breadstick.

(FEE say la)
plural: ficelles (same pronunciation; silent "s")

White

It's the night BEFORE Bake Day (p. 58). As usual, you're going to pull 1/2 cup mother from your Refrigerator Mother, feed her 3/8 cup flour and 1/4 cup water, stir/cover, and put her back until next week.

To the 1/2 cup mother now in your *Glasslock* bowl that's about to become "activated batter," you'll add 3/8 cup flour and 1/4 cup water; stir/cover.

It's Bake Day. Rise and shine! Feed your activated batter 3/8 cup flour and 1/4 cup water; stir/cover.
Two to three hours later, it's ready to go to work for you.

Cheese Mixture

Parmesan Cheese (shredded)	Asiago Cheese (shredded)	Gruyère Cheese (shredded)
1/4 cup	1/4 cup	1/4 cup

Depending on the type of flour you're using, follow the amounts in the chart below.

	Activated Batter	Water	Salt	Flour (same type as mother)	Ice Cubes (divided)	Egg Whites	Sea-Salt Flakes (divided)
White	1 1/2 cups	1 cup	1 1/2 t	2 3/4–3 1/4 cups	2 cups	1	1 t
Kamut	1 1/2 cups	1 cup	1 1/2 t	2 1/4–2 3/4 cups	2 cups	1	1 t
Sprouted	1 1/2 cups	1 cup	1 1/2 t	2 1/2–3 cups	2 cups	1	1 t
Einkorn	1 1/2 cups	1 cup	1 1/2 t	4 3/4–5 1/4 cups	2 cups	1	1 t
Einka	1 1/2 cups	1 cup	1 1/2 t	4–4 1/2 cups	2 cups	1	1 t

1. Prepare cheese mixture: Combine all cheeses in a small bowl.

2. To the batter in your bowl, add water, salt, and cheese mixture; mix well. Starting with the smallest amount of flour in the chart, reserve 1 cup of it for kneading and add the rest of it to the bowl with the batter; mix until a stiff, tacky dough forms. Let rest 5 minutes.

3. Dust a clean work surface with reserved flour and scoop dough out of bowl. As you begin to work in the reserved flour, resist the urge to add more flour, as it will produce a dense loaf. Instead, very lightly coat your hands with cooking oil to prevent dough from sticking to your hands. If dough is still too sticky after reserved flour has been worked in, begin working in another 1/2 cup of flour. Continue to knead until dough is smooth, pliable, and slightly tacky (about 8 minutes).

4. Wash and dry bowl and coat with safflower oil. Shape dough into a ball and add to bowl. Cover bowl with its lid and let rest in a warm place (70–73°F) for 30 minutes.

5. After 30 minutes, remove lid. Starting at the edge of the bowl, lift a portion of the dough toward the center of the bowl using a bowl scraper. Rotate the bowl, lift another portion, and fold it toward the center. Repeat until all edges have been folded toward the center (6–8 total folds). Cover bowl with lid and let rest again in a warm place (70–73°F) for 30 minutes. Repeat fold/rest two more times. Now, you're done with the folding process that conditions the dough so it rises well (step 7).

6. After the last 30 minutes, lightly dust a clean work surface with flour and scoop dough from bowl using the bowl scraper. Divide dough into 8 equal portions and roll each portion into a 15" rope.

7. Line two baker's sheets with parchment paper. Using a baguette board, transfer ropes to prepared baking sheets, four to a sheet, parallel to the longest side of the sheet, allowing plenty of room between each rope. Cover with a flour-sack cotton towel and let rise for 30 minutes.

8. Before bread finishes its 30-minute rise, move an oven rack to the center of the oven and another to the bottom. Place an enameled cast-iron Dutch oven on the bottom rack. Preheat oven to 425°F.

9. Working with one baking sheet of ficelles at a time, use a bread lame to make a swift, superficial slash down the length of each ficelle. Place baking sheet in oven. Add 1 cup ice cubes to the enameled cast-iron Dutch oven (Why? See p. 216.). Bake for 10 minutes.

10. Meanwhile, in a small bowl. Combine egg white and 1 t water and mix until frothy. After ficelles have baked 10 minutes, remove from oven, brush with egg-white wash, and sprinkle with 1/2 t sea-salt flakes. Return to oven and bake an additional 5 minutes, or until internal temperature reaches 190°F. Remove from oven and transfer to a cooling rack. Repeat for second baking sheet.

White
Rice

Quinoa

Tip: To brown the surface of white- or brown-rice ficelle (quinoa browns beautifully on its own), dissolve 1/2 t baking soda in 1/4 cup water. Transfer to a spray bottle and mist tops of loaves before baking.

It's the night BEFORE Bake Day (p. 58). As usual, you're going to pull 1/2 cup mother from your Refrigerator Mother, feed her 3/8 cup flour and 1/4 cup water, stir/cover, and put her back until next week.

To the 1/2 cup mother now in your *Glasslock* bowl that's about to become "activated batter," you'll add 3/8 cup flour and 1/4 cup water; stir/cover.

It's Bake Day. Rise and shine! Feed your activated batter 3/8 cup flour and 1/4 cup water; stir/cover. Two to three hours later, it's ready to go to work for you.

Cheese Mixture

Parmesan Cheese (shredded)	Asiago Cheese (shredded)	Gruyère Cheese (shredded)
1/4 cup	1/4 cup	1/4 cup

Depending on the type of flour you're using, follow the amounts in the chart below.

	Activated Batter	Water	Salt	Flour (same type as mother)	B.F.M. Rice Starch*	Ice Cubes	Egg Whites	Sea-Salt Flakes (divided)
White Rice	1 1/2 cups	1 1/2 cups	1 1/2 t	2 cups	1/2 cup	2 cups	1	1 t
Brown Rice	1 1/2 cups	1 1/2 cups	1 1/2 t	3 1/2 cups	3/4 cup	2 cups	1	1 t
Quinoa	1 1/2 cups	1 1/2 cups	1 1/2 t	5 cups	none	2 cups	1	1 t

*Barron Flour Mill rice starch, p. 195

1. Prepare cheese mixture: Combine all cheeses in a small bowl.

2. To the batter in your bowl, add water, salt, and cheese mixture; mix well.

3. Add about half the required flour (and the rice starch, if using). Mix until a tacky dough forms; let rest 5 minutes.

4. Mix in remaining flour (dough may seem dry, but will moisten and come together during conditioning).

5. Cover bowl with its lid and let rest in a warm place (70–73°F) for 30 minutes.

6. After the last 30 minutes, remove lid. Starting at the edge of the bowl, lift a portion of the dough toward the center of the bowl using a bowl scraper. Rotate the bowl, lift another portion, and fold it toward the center. Repeat until all edges have been folded toward the center (6–8 total folds). Cover bowl with lid and let rest again in a warm place (70–73°F) for 30 minutes. Repeat fold/rest two more times. Now, you're done with the folding process that conditions the dough so it rises well (step 8).

7. After the last 30 minutes, lightly dust a clean work surface with flour and scoop dough from bowl using the bowl scraper. Divide dough into 8 equal portions and roll each portion into a 15" rope, smoothing out imperfections as you work.

8. Line two baker's sheets with parchment paper. Using a baguette board, transfer ropes to prepared baking sheets, four to a sheet, parallel to the longest side of the sheet, allowing plenty of room between each rope. Cover with a flour-sack cotton towel and let rise for 30 minutes.

9. Before bread finishes its 30-minute rise, move an oven rack to the center of the oven and another to the bottom. Place an enameled cast-iron Dutch oven on the bottom rack. Preheat oven to 425°F.

10. Working with one baking sheet of ficelles at a time, spray ficelles with baking-soda mixture, if using (see tip). Place one baking sheet in oven. Add 1 cup ice cubes to enameled cast-iron Dutch oven (Why? See p. 216.). Bake for 15 minutes.

11. Meanwhile, in a small bowl. Combine egg white and 1 t water and mix until frothy. After ficelles have baked 15 minutes, remove from oven, brush with egg-white wash, and sprinkle with 1/2 t sea-salt flakes. Return to oven and bake an additional 5 minutes, or until internal temperature reaches 190°F. Remove from oven and transfer to a cooling rack. Repeat for second baking sheet.

Proofing Time: 2 hours, 30 minutes   Bake Time: 40 minutes   Makes: Eight 15" ficelles

KOULOURI

This popular Greek street bread mimics a bagel, but with a twist all its own, literally. Right before being dipped in sesame seeds, it's dipped in grape must (from the Latin *vinum mustum*, "young wine"). Grape must is created during the first step in winemaking, when whole grapes, skins, seeds, and stems are mashed together. Must is thick with particulate matter and comes in shades of brown or dark purple. It's regularly used in Greek cooking and is available online.

(COOL or ray)
plural: koulouria (COOL or ree ah)

Sprouted

It's the night BEFORE Bake Day (p. 58). As usual, you're going to pull 1/2 cup mother from your Refrigerator Mother, feed her 3/8 cup flour and 1/4 cup water, stir/cover, and put her back until next week.

To the 1/2 cup mother now in your *Glasslock* bowl that's about to become "activated batter," you'll add 3/8 cup flour and 1/4 cup water; stir/cover.

It's Bake Day. Rise and shine! Feed your activated batter 3/8 cup flour and 1/4 cup water; stir/cover. Two to three hours later, it's ready to go to work for you.

Depending on the type of flour you're using, follow the amounts in the chart below.

	Activated Batter	Milk	Eggs	Olive Oil	Honey	Salt	Flour (same type as mother)
White	1 1/2 cups	1/2 cup	2	2 T	2 T	1 1/2 t	3 1/2–3 3/4 cups
Kamut	1 1/2 cups	1/2 cup	2	2 T	2 T	1 1/2 t	3–3 1/4 cups
Sprouted	1 1/2 cups	1/2 cup	2	2 T	2 T	1 1/2 t	3–3 1/4 cups
Einkorn	1 1/2 cups	1/2 cup	2	2 T	2 T	1 1/2 t	4 1/4–4 1/2 cups
Einka	1 1/2 cups	1/2 cup	2	2 T	2 T	1 1/2 t	3 3/4–4 cups

Sesame Coating

Sesame Seeds	Water	Grape Must
1 cup	1/4 cup	2 T

1. To the batter in your bowl, add milk, eggs, olive oil, honey, and salt; mix well. Starting with the smallest amount of flour in the chart, reserve 1 cup of it for kneading and add the rest of it to the bowl with the batter; mix until a stiff, tacky dough forms. Let rest 5 minutes.

2. Dust a clean work surface with reserved flour and scoop dough out of bowl. As you begin to work in the reserved flour, resist the urge to add more flour, as it will produce a dense loaf. Instead, very lightly coat your hands with cooking oil to prevent dough from sticking to your hands. If dough is still too sticky after reserved flour has been worked in, begin working in another 1/4 cup of flour. Continue to knead until dough is smooth, pliable, and slightly tacky (about 8 minutes).

3. Wash and dry bowl and coat with olive oil. Shape dough into a ball and add to bowl. Cover bowl with its lid and let rest in a warm place (70–73°F) for 30 minutes.

4. After 30 minutes, remove lid. Starting at the edge of the bowl, lift a portion of the dough toward the center of the bowl using a bowl scraper. Rotate the bowl, lift another portion, and fold it toward the center. Repeat until all edges have been folded toward the center (6–8 total folds). Cover bowl with lid and let rest again in a warm place (70–73°F) for 30 minutes. Repeat fold/rest two more times. Now, you're done with the folding process that conditions the dough so it rises well (step 8).

5. Meanwhile, prepare Sesame Coating: Add sesame seeds to a large skillet. Toast over medium-low heat, stirring frequently until fragrant and golden brown. Remove from heat and transfer to a small bowl. In another small bowl, combine water and grape must; mix well and set aside.

6. Line a baker's sheet with parchment paper.

7. After the last 30 minutes, lightly dust a clean work surface with flour and scoop dough from bowl using the bowl scraper. Divide dough into 8 equal portions and roll each portion into a 24"-long rope. Place ropes on a lightly floured surface.

8. Fold each rope in half, and twist into a spiral. Bring ends together to form a circle and tuck the raw end into the loop on the opposite end. Dip one koulouri into grape-must mixture, and flip over to completely coat. Dip in sesame seeds, and flip over to completely coat. Place on prepared baking sheet and repeat with remaining koulouria. Once all koulouria have been coated in sesame seeds, cover with a flour-sack cotton towel and let rise for 30 minutes.

9. Before bread finishes its 30-minute rise, move an oven rack to the center of the oven. Preheat oven to 400°F.

10. Remove flour-sack cotton towel and bake for 20 minutes, or until internal temperature reaches 205°F.

Proofing Time: 2 hours, 30 minutes   Bake Time: 20 minutes   Makes: Eight koulouria

Einka

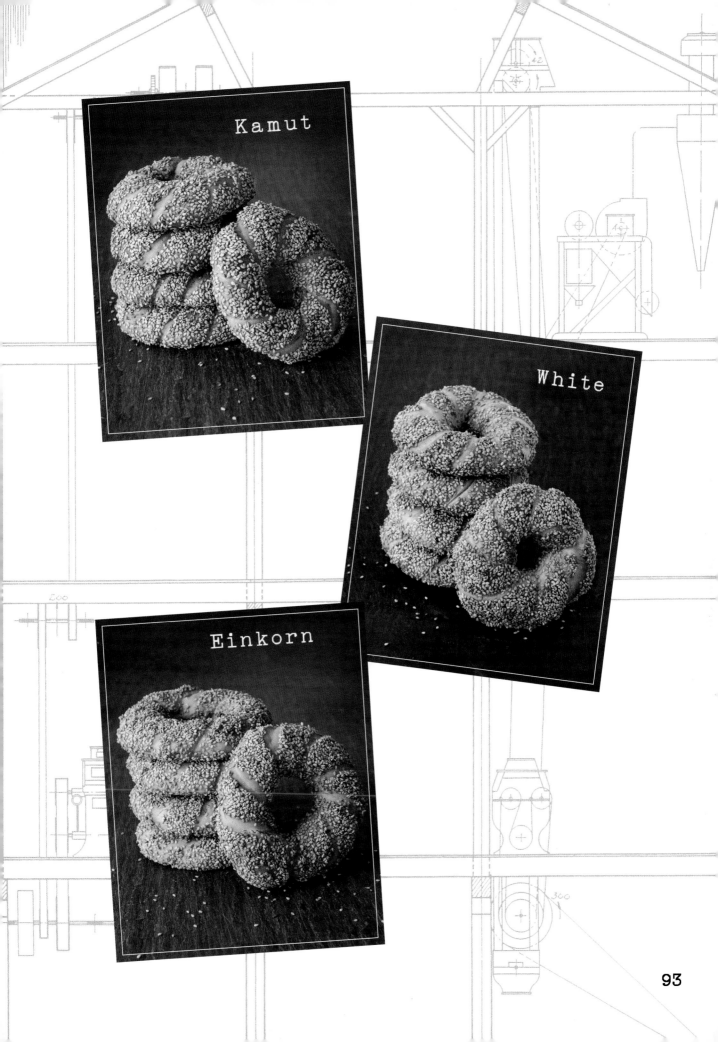

Kamut

White

Einkorn

93

FOUGASSE

(FOO gah sa)
plural: fougasses
(same pronunciation;
silent "s")

Kamut

In French cuisine,
fougasse is similar to
Italian focaccia. Flat and
crusty, this leaf-shaped
pull-apart bread looks
picture perfect in the
center of a table whenever
people gather together to
break bread.

It's the night BEFORE Bake Day (p. 58). As usual, you're going to pull 1/2 cup mother from your Refrigerator Mother, feed her 3/8 cup flour and 1/4 cup water, stir/cover, and put her back until next week.

To the 1/2 cup mother now in your *Glasslock* bowl that's about to become "activated batter," you'll add 3/8 cup flour and 1/4 cup water; stir/cover.

It's Bake Day. Rise and shine! Feed your activated batter 3/8 cup flour and 1/4 cup water; stir/cover. Two to three hours later, it's ready to go to work for you.

Depending on the type of flour you're using, follow the amounts in the chart below.

	Activated Batter	Water	Salt	Flour (same type as mother)	Ice Cubes
White	1 1/2 cups	1 cup	1 1/2 t	2 3/4–3 1/4 cups	1 cup
Kamut	1 1/2 cups	1 cup	1 1/2 t	2 1/4–2 3/4 cups	1 cup
Sprouted	1 1/2 cups	1 cup	1 1/2 t	2 1/2–3 cups	1 cup
Einkorn	1 1/2 cups	1 cup	1 1/2 t	4 3/4–5 1/4 cups	1 cup
Einka	1 1/2 cups	1 cup	1 1/2 t	4–4 1/2 cups	1 cup

Herb Coating

Egg Whites	Sea-Salt Flakes	Dried Rosemary	Dried Basil	Dried Thyme
1	1 1/4 t	1/2 t	1/2 t	1/4 t

1. To the batter in your bowl, add water and salt; mix well. Starting with the smallest amount of flour in the chart, reserve 1 cup of it for kneading and add the rest of it to the bowl with the batter; mix until a stiff, tacky dough forms. Let rest 5 minutes.

2. Dust a clean work surface with reserved flour and scoop dough out of bowl. As you begin to work in the reserved flour, resist the urge to add more flour, as it will produce a dense loaf. Instead, very lightly coat your hands with cooking oil to prevent dough from sticking to your hands. If dough is still too sticky after reserved flour has been worked in, begin working in another 1/2 cup of flour. Continue to knead until dough is smooth, pliable, and slightly tacky (about 8 minutes).

3. Wash and dry bowl and coat with safflower oil. Shape dough into a ball and add to bowl. Cover bowl with its lid and let rest in a warm place (70–73°F) for 30 minutes.

4. After 30 minutes, remove lid. Starting at the edge of the bowl, lift a portion of the dough toward the center of the bowl using a bowl scraper. Rotate the bowl, lift another portion, and fold it toward the center. Repeat until all edges have been folded toward the center (6–8 total folds). Cover bowl with lid and let rest again in a warm place (70–73°F) for 30 minutes. Repeat fold/rest two more times. Now, you're done with the folding process that conditions the dough so it rises well (step 7).

5. After the last 30 minutes, lightly dust a sheet of parchment paper with flour and scoop dough from bowl onto parchment, using the bowl scraper.

6. Lightly dust surface of dough with flour and press into a leaf shape, roughly 13" long and 11" wide at its widest point.

7. Using a pastry wheel, cut a vein down the center of the leaf. Gently pull each side away from the center vein to make it more pronounced. Next, using the pastry wheel cut 3 angled lines on each side of the center vein to form a leaf pattern. Gently pull each slit open to make them more pronounced. Once all leaf veins have been cut, cover fougasse with a flour-sack cotton towel and let rise for 45 minutes.

8. Before bread finishes its 45-minute rise, move an oven rack to the center of the oven and another to the bottom. Place an enameled cast-iron Dutch oven on the bottom rack and a 15"-square baking stone on the center rack. Preheat oven to 425°F.

9. Slide pizza peel under parchment paper and loaf. Slide bread and parchment paper off pizza peel onto baking stone. Add ice cubes to enameled cast-iron Dutch oven. (Why? See p. 216.) Bake for 20 minutes.

10. Meanwhile, prepare Herb Coating: In a small bowl, combine egg white and 1 t water and mix until frothy. In another small bowl, combine sea-salt flakes, rosemary, basil, and thyme. After fougasse has baked 20 minutes, remove from oven, using the pizza peel. Brush with egg-white wash and sprinkle with herb coating. Return to oven and bake an additional 5 minutes, or until internal temperature reaches 190°F.

Proofing Time: 2 hours, 45 minutes   Bake Time: 25 minutes   Makes: One 11" x 13" fougasse

To make Kale Chips, preheat oven to 300°F. Remove stems from about 1 pound of kale and tear leaves into pieces. Wash leaves well and dry completely using a salad spinner. Add to a large bowl and toss with 2 T olive oil and 1/4 t salt. Arrange kale on a baker's sheet in a single layer. Bake for 30 minutes, or until crisp, stirring halfway through. Remove from oven, cool slightly, and eat as a snack or use as a topping on soup.

Sprouted

Einkorn

Einka

White

GLUTEN-FREE FOUGASSE

White Rice

Brown Rice

It's the night BEFORE Bake Day (p. 58). As usual, you're going to pull 1/2 cup mother from your Refrigerator Mother, feed her 3/8 cup flour and 1/4 cup water, stir/cover, and put her back until next week.

To the 1/2 cup mother now in your *Glasslock* bowl that's about to become "activated batter," you'll add 3/8 cup flour and 1/4 cup water; stir/cover.

It's Bake Day. Rise and shine! Feed your activated batter 3/8 cup flour and 1/4 cup water; stir/cover. Two to three hours later, it's ready to go to work for you.

Depending on the type of flour you're using, follow the amounts in the chart below.

	Activated Batter	Water	Salt	Flour (same type as mother)	B.F.M. Rice Starch*	Ice Cubes
White Rice	1 1/2 cups	1 1/2 cups	1 1/2 t	2 cups	1/2 cup	1 cup
Brown Rice	1 1/2 cups	1 1/2 cups	1 1/2 t	3 1/2 cups	3/4 cup	1 cup
Quinoa	1 1/2 cups	1 1/2 cups	1 1/2 t	5 cups	none	1 cup

*Barron Flour Mill rice starch, p. 195

Herb Coating

Egg Whites	Sea-Salt Flakes	Dried Rosemary	Dried Basil	Dried Thyme
1	1 1/4 t	1/2 t	1/2 t	1/4 t

1. To the batter in your bowl, add water and salt; mix well.

2. Add about half the required flour (and the rice starch, if using). Mix until a tacky dough forms; let rest 5 minutes.

3. Mix in remaining flour (dough may seem dry, but it will moisten and come together during proofing).

4. Cover bowl with its lid and let rest in a warm place (70–73°F) for 30 minutes.

5. After 30 minutes, remove lid. Starting at the edge of the bowl, lift a portion of the dough toward the center of the bowl using a bowl scraper. Rotate the bowl, lift another portion, and fold it toward the center. Repeat until all edges have been folded toward the center (6–8 total folds). Cover bowl with lid and let rest again in a warm place (70–73°F) for 30 minutes. Repeat fold/rest two more times. Now, you're done with the folding process that conditions the dough so it rises well (step 8).

Quinoa

6. After the last 30 minutes, lightly dust a sheet of parchment paper with flour and scoop dough from bowl onto parchment, using the bowl scraper.

7. Lightly dust surface of dough with flour and press into a leaf shape, roughly 13" long and 11" wide at its widest point.

8. Using the blunt end of a wooden skewer, cut a vein down the center of the leaf. Gently push each side away from the center vein to make it more pronounced. Next, using the wooden skewer, cut 3 angled lines on each side of the center vein to form a leaf pattern. Gently push each slit open to make them more pronounced. Once all leaf veins have been shaped, cover fougasse with a flour-sack cotton towel and let rise for 45 minutes.

9. Before bread finishes its 45-minute rise, move an oven rack to the center of the oven and another to the bottom. Place an enameled cast-iron Dutch oven on the bottom rack and a 15"-square baking stone on the center rack. Preheat oven to 425°F.

10. Spray fougasse with baking-soda mixture, if using (see tip). Slide pizza peel under parchment paper and loaf. Slide bread and parchment paper off pizza peel onto baking stone. Add ice cubes to enameled cast-iron Dutch oven. (Why? See p. 216.) Bake for 20 minutes.

11. Meanwhile, prepare Herb Coating: In small bowl, combine egg white and 1 t water and mix until frothy. In another small bowl, combine sea-salt flakes, rosemary, basil, and thyme. After fougasse has baked 20 minutes, remove from oven, using the pizza peel. Brush with egg-white wash and sprinkle with herb coating. Return to oven and bake an additional 5 minutes, or until internal temperature reaches 190°F.

Tip: To brown the surface of white- or brown-rice fougasse (quinoa browns beautifully on its own), dissolve 1/2 t baking soda in 1/4 cup water. Transfer to a spray bottle and mist tops of loaves before baking.

Proofing Time: 2 hours, 45 minutes   Bake Time: 25 minutes   Makes: One 11" x 13" fougasse

Ciabatta, or slipper bread, is a rustic Italian bread. It's a moist bread with an irregular oval shape. It has a light golden crust and a soft interior with large, irregular holes.

(chah BAH tah)

plural: ciabattas (chah BAH tahs) or ciabatte (chah BAH tay)

Einkorn

It's the night BEFORE Bake Day (p. 58). As usual, you're going to pull 1/2 cup mother from your Refrigerator Mother, feed her 3/8 cup flour and 1/4 cup water, stir/cover, and put her back until next week.

To the 1/2 cup mother now in your *Glasslock* bowl that's about to become "activated batter," you'll add 3/8 cup flour and 1/4 cup water; stir/cover.

It's Bake Day. Rise and shine! Feed your activated batter 3/8 cup flour and 1/4 cup water; stir/cover. Two to three hours later, it's ready to go to work for you.

Depending on the type of flour you're using, follow the amounts in the chart below.

	Activated Batter	Water	Milk	Salt	Flour (same type as mother)	Ice Cubes
White	1 1/2 cups	1 cup	1/3 cup	1 1/2 t	3 1/2 cups	1 cup
Kamut	1 1/2 cups	1 cup	1/3 cup	1 1/2 t	3 cups	1 cup
Sprouted	1 1/2 cups	1 cup	1/3 cup	1 1/2 t	3 cups	1 cup
Einkorn	1 1/2 cups	1 cup	1/3 cup	1 1/2 t	4 3/4 cups	1 cup
Einka	1 1/2 cups	1 cup	1/3 cup	1 1/2 t	4 1/4 cups	1 cup

1. To the batter in your bowl, add water, milk, and salt; mix well.

2. Add flour to a large bowl or stand mixer fitted with a flat beater. Add batter mixture to the flour and mix until a smooth, sticky dough forms.

3. Wash and dry bowl and coat with safflower oil. Scoop dough into oiled bowl, cover bowl with its lid and let rest in a warm place (70–73°F) for 30 minutes.

4. After 30 minutes, remove lid. Starting at the edge of the bowl, lift a portion of the dough toward the center of the bowl using a bowl scraper. Rotate the bowl, lift another portion, and fold it toward the center. Repeat until all edges have been folded toward the center (6–8 total folds). Cover bowl with lid and let rest again in a warm place (70–73°F) for 30 minutes. Repeat fold/rest two more times. Now, you're done with the folding process that conditions the dough so it rises well (step 7).

5. After the last 30 minutes, place a sheet of parchment paper on an inverted baker's sheet and lightly dust with flour; set aside.

6. Generously dust a clean work surface with flour and scoop dough out of bowl. Lightly dust top of dough with flour. Gently press dough into an 8" x 16" rectangle. From the 16" end, fold dough into thirds using a dough scraper. From the 8" side, fold dough in half. Using a dough scraper, transfer dough to prepared parchment paper.

7. Gently press dough into a 6" x 12" rectangle. Cover with a flour-sack cotton towel and let rise for 30 minutes.

8. Before bread finishes its 30-minute rise, move an oven rack to the center of the oven and another to the bottom. Place an enameled cast-iron Dutch oven on the bottom rack and a 15"-square baking stone on the center rack. Preheat oven to 450°F.

9. Slide pizza peel under parchment paper and loaf. Slide bread and parchment paper off pizza peel onto baking stone. Add ice cubes to enameled cast-iron Dutch oven. (Why? See p. 216.)

10. Bake for 20–25 minutes, or until internal temperature reaches 200–205°F. Remove from oven and transfer to a cooling rack.

Einka

Einka

To make ciabatta sandwich rolls, divide dough into 8 equal portions. Shape each portion into a 3 1/2" x 4" rectangle and place on an inverted baker's sheet lined with parchment paper. Cover with a flour-sack cotton towel and let rest for 30 minutes. Follow steps 8–9 of ciabatta recipe. Bake for 15–18 minutes, or until internal temperature reaches 200–205°F. Remove from oven and transfer to a cooling rack.

Kamut

Sprouted

White

(SKAL ee—think scallywag without the wag)
this bread is usually referred to in the plural form; singular:
scala (SKAL ah)

Once we discovered how much we liked sesame-covered koulouria (Greek bagels, p. 90), we knew we wanted more of the same, but in a loaf form. Thankfully, it's a long-standing traditional bread popular not just in Italy, but in Boston, Massachusetts, as well. Scala is an Italian loaf of braided bread drenched in sesame seeds. It has a soft interior with a chewy, full-bodied, brown crust that's bursting with flavor.

White

It's the night BEFORE Bake Day (p. 58). As usual,

you're going to pull 1/2 cup mother from your Refrigerator Mother, feed her 3/8 cup flour and 1/4 cup water, stir/cover, and put her back until next week.

To the 1/2 cup mother now in your *Glasslock* bowl that's about to become "activated batter," you'll add 3/8 cup flour and 1/4 cup water; stir/cover.

It's Bake Day. Rise and shine! Feed your activated batter 3/8 cup flour and 1/4 cup water; stir/cover.
Two to three hours later, it's ready to go to work for you.

Depending on the type of flour you're using, follow the amounts in the chart below.

	Activated Batter	Water	Milk	Salt	Flour (same type as mother)	Egg Whites	Sesame Seeds (divided)
White	1 1/2 cups	1 cup	1/3 cup	1 1/2 t	4 1/4 cups	1	1/2 cup
Kamut	1 1/2 cups	1 cup	1/3 cup	1 1/2 t	3 1/2 cups	1	1/2 cup
Sprouted	1 1/2 cups	1 cup	1/3 cup	1 1/2 t	4 1/2 cups	1	1/2 cup
Einkorn	1 1/2 cups	1 cup	1/3 cup	1 1/2 t	5 1/4 cups	1	1/2 cup
Einka	1 1/2 cups	1 cup	1/3 cup	1 1/2 t	5 cups	1	1/2 cup

1. To the batter in your bowl, add water, milk, and salt; mix well. Reserve 1 cup flour for kneading and add the rest of it to the bowl with the batter; mix until a stiff, tacky dough forms. Let rest 5 minutes.

2. Dust a clean work surface with reserved flour and scoop dough out of bowl. As you begin to work in the reserved flour, resist the urge to add more flour, as it will produce a dense loaf. Instead, very lightly coat your hands with cooking oil to prevent dough from sticking to your hands. Continue to knead until dough is smooth, pliable, and slightly tacky (about 8 minutes).

3. Wash and dry bowl and coat with safflower oil. Shape dough into a ball and add to bowl. Cover bowl with its lid and let rest in a warm place (70–73°F) for 30 minutes.

4. After 30 minutes, remove lid. Starting at the edge of the bowl, lift a portion of the dough toward the center of the bowl using a bowl scraper. Rotate the bowl, lift another portion, and fold it toward the center. Repeat until all edges have been folded toward the center (6–8 total folds). Cover bowl with lid and let rest again in a warm place (70–73°F) for 30 minutes. Repeat fold/rest two more times. Now, you're done with the folding process that conditions the dough so it rises well (step 8).

5. After the last 30 minutes, lightly dust a clean work surface with flour and scoop dough from bowl using the bowl scraper. Divide dough into 3 equal portions and roll each portion into a 12"-long rope. Place ropes on a lightly floured surface and set aside.

6. Lightly dust a sheet of parchment paper with flour and set aside.

7. In a small bowl, combine egg white and 1 t water and mix until frothy. Add 1/4 cup sesame seeds to a baker's sheet and shake sheet to spread out seeds. Brush the top of one rope with egg-white wash and roll in sesame seeds. Brush the bottom of the rope with egg-white wash and turn to coat in sesame seeds. Transfer coated rope to prepared parchment paper. Repeat process with remaining ropes, adding more sesame seeds to baking sheet as needed.

8. Pinch the three ropes together at one end and braid the ropes together. Tuck each end of the braid under, cover with a flour-sack cotton towel, and let rise for 45 minutes.

9. Before bread finishes its 45-minute rise, move an oven rack to the center of the oven. Place a 15"-square baking stone on the center rack. Preheat oven to 375°F.

10. Slide pizza peel under parchment paper and loaf. Slide bread and parchment paper off pizza peel onto baking stone. Bake for 45 minutes, or until internal temperature reaches 200–205°F. Remove from oven and transfer to a cooling rack.

Proofing Time: 2 hours, 45 minutes   Bake Time: 45 minutes   Makes: One 12" scali

105

Kamut

Sprouted

Einkorn

Einka

This ceremonial bread, traditionally eaten on Shabbat and major Jewish holidays, is enriched with eggs and a little bit of sweetener.

(HALL lah)

plural: challahs (HALL lahs)

Einkorn

White

It's the night BEFORE Bake Day (p. 58). As usual, you're going to pull 1/2 cup mother from your Refrigerator Mother, feed her 3/8 cup flour and 1/4 cup water, stir/cover, and put her back until next week.

To the 1/2 cup mother now in your *Glasslock* bowl that's about to become "activated batter," you'll add 3/8 cup flour and 1/4 cup water; stir/cover.

It's Bake Day. Rise and shine! Feed your activated batter 3/8 cup flour and 1/4 cup water; stir/cover. Two to three hours later, it's ready to go to work for you.

Depending on the type of flour you're using, follow the amounts in the chart below.

	Activated Batter	Water	Honey	Olive Oil	Salt	Eggs (divided)	Flour (same type as mother)
White	1 1/2 cups	1/2 cup	1/4 cup	2 T	1 1/2 t	4	4 1/2–4 3/4 cups
Kamut	1 1/2 cups	1/2 cup	1/4 cup	2 T	1 1/2 t	4	3 3/4–4 cups
Sprouted	1 1/2 cups	1/2 cup	1/4 cup	2 T	1 1/2 t	4	4 1/2–4 3/4 cups
Einkorn	1 1/2 cups	1/2 cup	1/4 cup	2 T	1 1/2 t	4	5 1/4–5 1/2 cups
Einka	1 1/2 cups	1/2 cup	1/4 cup	2 T	1 1/2 t	4	4 1/4–4 1/2 cups

1. To the batter in your bowl, add water, honey, olive oil, and salt; mix well. Add 3 whole eggs and 1 egg yolk (reserve white for egg-white wash); mix well.

2. Reserve 1 cup flour for kneading and add the rest of it to the bowl with the batter; mix until a stiff, tacky dough forms. Let rest 5 minutes.

3. Dust a clean work surface with reserved flour and scoop dough out of bowl. As you begin to work in the reserved flour, resist the urge to add more flour, as it will produce a dense loaf. Instead, very lightly coat your hands with cooking oil to prevent dough from sticking to your hands. If dough is still too sticky after reserved flour has been worked in, begin working in another 1/4 cup of flour. Continue to knead until dough is smooth, pliable, and slightly tacky (about 8 minutes).

4. Wash and dry bowl and coat with olive oil. Shape dough into a ball and add to bowl. Cover bowl with its lid and let rest in a warm place (70–73°F) for 30 minutes.

5. After 30 minutes, remove lid. Starting at the edge of the bowl, lift a portion of the dough toward the center of the bowl using a bowl scraper. Rotate the bowl, lift another portion, and fold it toward the center. Repeat until all edges have been folded toward the center (6–8 total folds). Cover bowl with lid and let rest again in a warm place (70–73°F) for 30 minutes. Repeat fold/rest two more times. Now, you're done with the folding process that conditions the dough so it rises well (step 9).

6. Lightly dust a sheet of parchment paper with flour and set aside.

7. After the last 30 minutes, lightly dust a clean work surface with flour and scoop dough from bowl using the bowl scraper. Divide dough into 6 equal portions and roll each portion into an 18"-long strand. Transfer strands to prepared parchment paper.

8. To braid the loaf, arrange strands on parchment paper so they are all parallel. To create a six-strand braid, alternate these movements with the outermost strand on each side:
   Right side: Over two ropes, under one.
   Left side: Under two ropes, over one.

9. Once loaf is braided, tuck ends under and pinch to seal. Using a pizza peel, transfer loaf and parchment to a baker's sheet, cover with a flour-sack cotton towel, and let rise for 45 minutes.

10. Before bread finishes its 45-minute rise, move an oven rack to the center of the oven. Preheat oven to 400°F.

11. Remove flour-sack cotton towel and bake loaf for 20 minutes.

12. While bread is baking, whisk reserved egg white with 1 t cold water together until frothy; strain mixture through a fine-mesh sieve to remove clumps (this creates a smooth, glossy finish on the challah). Remove bread from oven, brush with egg-white wash, and bake for 5 minutes.

13. After 5 minutes, cover loaf with foil (this will prevent over-browning) and bake an additional 15 minutes, or until internal temperature reaches 200–205°F.

Proofing Time: 2 hours, 45 minutes   Bake Time: 40 minutes   Makes: One 16" challah

To make Sweet Cream Syrup, add 1 1/2 cups of cream to a medium saucepan. Bring to a low simmer over low heat, whisking frequently, until the volume is reduced by half (this should take about 20 minutes). Watch it carefully—the cream is prone to bubbling and will spill over onto your stovetop if not watched diligently. Whisk in 1 T sugar and continue to cook until the sugar is dissolved, then remove from heat.

Sprouted

The landscape surrounding my farm is dotted with abandoned grain elevators—storage towers containing a conveyor that scooped up grain from a lower level, depositing it onto a growing pile of grain or corn that eventually reached the top of the elevator. Gravity fed on its way back down, the grain, on an as-needed basis, would be carted to local flour mills. Once it arrived at the Barron Flour Mill (pictured here is one of the horse-drawn carts that were used), the grain would be shoveled into a floor grate, where a conveyor system once again lifted it up, this time to be processed into flour or animal feed. We still use one of the original milling machines to crack garbanzo beans, wheat, and corn.

Einka

Kamut

111

Tip: For breads that don't call for an egg-white wash, you might like rubbing fresh-from-the-oven loaves with butter. The butter helps even out the color on the crust, removes light residual flour blemishes, and gives loaves a subtle luster.

Sprouted

Tip: To make a traditional mounded-top loaf instead, gently press dough out into an 8" x 10" rectangle. Beginning from an 8" side for the *Jamie Oliver* tin, or a 10" side for the *Norpro* pan, roll dough up jelly-roll style. Pinch seams together at the bottom and sides. Place dough into prepared loaf pan. Cover with plastic wrap and let rise in a warm place for 2 hours, or until dough is level with the top of the pan. Remove plastic wrap. Using a bread lame, make a 1/8"-deep slash down the length of the loaf and bake as recipe directs.

Norpro pan

4.5" wide

3" tall

10" long

Jamie Oliver tin

5" wide

4" tall

8" long

White

It's the night BEFORE Bake Day (p. 58). As usual, you're going to pull 1/2 cup mother from your Refrigerator Mother, feed her 3/8 cup flour and 1/4 cup water, stir/cover, and put her back until next week.

To the 1/2 cup mother now in your *Glasslock* bowl that's about to become "activated batter," you'll add 3/8 cup flour and 1/4 cup water; stir/cover.

It's Bake Day. Rise and shine! Feed your activated batter 3/8 cup flour and 1/4 cup water; stir/cover. Two to three hours later, it's ready to go to work for you.

Depending on the type of flour you're using, follow the amounts in the chart below.

	Activated Batter	Milk	Butter	Sugar	Salt	Eggs	Flour (same type as mother)
White	1 1/2 cups	1/2 cup	4 T	2 T	1 t	1	3 1/4 cups
Kamut	1 1/2 cups	1/2 cup	4 T	2 T	1 t	1	3 1/4 cups
Sprouted	1 1/2 cups	1/2 cup	4 T	2 T	1 t	1	3 1/4 cups
Einkorn	1 1/2 cups	1/2 cup	4 T	2 T	1 t	1	4 cups
Einka	1 1/2 cups	1/2 cup	4 T	2 T	1 t	1	4 cups

1. In a small saucepan over low heat, combine milk, butter, sugar, and salt. Cook until sugar dissolves and butter begins to melt. Using your digital thermometer, test to make sure the mixture isn't hotter than 100°F. Add milk mixture and egg to bowl with batter; mix until smooth.

2. Reserve 1/2 cup flour for kneading. Add remaining flour to bowl with batter and mix until a stiff, tacky dough forms. Dust a clean work surface with reserved flour and scoop dough out of bowl. Knead dough until smooth and pliable (about 5 minutes).

3. Wash and dry bowl and coat with butter. Shape dough into a ball, add to bowl, cover bowl with its lid, and let condition in a warm place (70–73°F) for 2 hours.

4. Lightly butter a *Norpro* 10" nonstick bread pan or a *Jamie Oliver* 1.5-liter nonstick loaf tin and set aside.

5. Lightly dust a clean work surface with flour and scoop dough from bowl using the bowl scraper. Divide dough into 4 equal portions. Shape each portion into a ball and place in prepared loaf pan, pushing balls together so they nestle in bottom of pan (if you prefer a traditional mounded loaf, see tip at left). Cover with plastic wrap and let rise in a warm place for 2 hours, or until dough is level with the top of the pan.

6. Before bread finishes its second rise, move an oven rack to the center of the oven. Preheat oven to 350°F.

7. Remove plastic wrap and bake for 30 minutes. Cover top of bread with foil to prevent over-browning and bake an additional 15 minutes, or until internal temperature reaches 200–205°F.

8. Cool slightly in pan, then transfer to a cooling rack to cool completely.

Sunbeam

BREAD WITH A BONUS

More Energy
More Nutrition
More Flavor

White

Kamut

Einka

Einkorn

White Rice

Tip: To brown the surface of white- or brown-rice sandwich loaves (quinoa browns beautifully on its own), dissolve 1/2 t baking soda in 1/4 cup water. Transfer to a spray bottle and mist tops of loaves before baking.

Quinoa

Brown Rice

It's the night BEFORE Bake Day (p. 58). As usual, you're going to pull 1/2 cup mother from your Refrigerator Mother, feed her 3/8 cup flour and 1/4 cup water, stir/cover, and put her back until next week.

To the 1/2 cup mother now in your *Glasslock* bowl that's about to become "activated batter," you'll add 3/8 cup flour and 1/4 cup water; stir/cover.

It's Bake Day. Rise and shine! Feed your activated batter 3/8 cup flour and 1/4 cup water; stir/cover. Two to three hours later, it's ready to go to work for you.

Depending on the type of flour you're using, follow the amounts in the chart below.

	Activated Batter	Milk	Eggs	Honey	Salt	Flour (same type as mother)	B.F.M. Rice Starch*
White Rice	1 1/2 cups	3 cups	2	1 T	1 1/2 t	2 cups	1/2 cup
Brown Rice	1 1/2 cups	2 1/2 cups	2	1 T	1 1/2 t	2 1/2 cups	1/2 cup
Quinoa	1 1/2 cups	2 1/2 cups	2	1 T	1 1/2 t	5 cups	none

*Barron Flour Mill rice starch, p. 195

1. Lightly butter a *Norpro* 10" x 4.5" nonstick bread pan or a *Jamie Oliver* 1.5-liter nonstick loaf tin and set aside.

2. To the batter in your bowl, add milk, eggs, honey, and salt; mix well.

3. Add flour (and rice starch, if using) and mix until a smooth, creamy batter forms.

4. Pour batter into prepared loaf pan, cover with plastic wrap, and let condition in a warm place (70–73°F) for 45 minutes. During this stage, the bread will not rise significantly. You may notice little bubbles forming at the surface. The bread will rise and dome as it bakes.

5. Before bread finishes its rest, move an oven rack to the center of the oven. Preheat oven to 350°F.

6. Remove plastic wrap and bake for 45 minutes. After 45 minutes, spray loaf with baking-soda mixture, if using (see tip, left). Bake an additional 30 minutes, or until internal temperature reaches 200–205°F.

7. Cool slightly in pan, then transfer to a cooling rack to cool completely.

Proofing Time: 45 minutes **Bake Time:** 1 hour, 15 minutes **Makes:** One loaf

aka Pullman Loaf

(panda ME) plural: pains de mie (same pronunciation; silent "s")

White

Pronounced *panda me*, with the *pan* part drawn out and the accent on *me*, pain de mie is a French loaf in a tight-fitting, rectangular pan with a lid. The pan constrains expansion of the dough, and the lid prevents much of a crust from forming. In France, it is sometimes sold sliced and packaged with the crust cut off entirely. The fat (butter) in pain de mie not only gives it a tighter crumb, it also helps keep it fresh longer and freeze well. Ideal for fancy sandwiches or for toasting, the English version is called a Pullman loaf (of railroad fame). Is it because the bread is shaped like a railway car, or is it because the loaves were uniform and took up less space in the kitchens of Pullman dining cars, or is it because it was easier to transport by rail when left in lidded, obviously stackable, pans? (continued on p. 120)

White

It's the night BEFORE Bake Day (p. 58). As usual, you're going to pull 1/2 cup mother from your Refrigerator Mother, feed her 3/8 cup flour and 1/4 cup water, stir/cover, and put her back until next week.

To the 1/2 cup mother now in your *Glasslock* bowl that's about to become "activated batter," you'll add 3/8 cup flour and 1/4 cup water; stir/cover.

It's Bake Day. Rise and shine! Feed your activated batter 3/8 cup flour and 1/4 cup water; stir/cover. Two to three hours later, it's ready to go to work for you.

Depending on the type of flour you're using, follow the amounts in the chart below.

	Activated Batter	Buttermilk	Butter	Honey	Salt	Egg Yolks	Flour (same type as mother)
White	1 1/2 cups	1 cup	2 T	1 T	1 1/2 t	3	3 cups
Kamut	1 1/2 cups	1 3/4 cups	3 T	1 T	1 1/2 t	3	3 1/2 cups
Sprouted	1 1/2 cups	1 1/2 cups	3 T	1 T	1 1/2 t	3	3 3/4 cups
Einkorn	1 1/2 cups	1 1/2 cups	3 T	1 T	1 1/2 t	3	4 1/2 cups
Einka	1 1/2 cups	1 1/2 cups	3 T	1 T	1 1/2 t	3	4 1/4 cups

1. In a small saucepan over low heat, combine buttermilk, butter, honey, and salt. Cook until honey dissolves and butter begins to melt. Using your digital thermometer, test to make sure the mixture isn't hotter than 100°F. Add buttermilk mixture and egg yolks to bowl with batter; mix until smooth.

2. Reserve 1/2 cup flour for kneading. Add remaining flour to bowl with batter and mix until a stiff, tacky dough forms. Dust a clean work surface with reserved flour and scoop dough out of bowl. Knead dough until smooth and pliable (about 5 minutes).

3. Wash and dry bowl and coat with butter. Shape dough into a ball, add to bowl, cover bowl with its lid, and let condition in a warm place (70–73°F) for 2 hours.

White

4. Lightly butter a *USA Pan* nonstick Pullman loaf pan and inside of lid and set aside.

5. After rising, deflate dough. Lightly dust a clean work surface with flour. Gently shape dough into a 13"-long log and place in prepared pan, smooth side up. Cover with plastic wrap and let rise in a warm place (70–73°F) for 2 hours, or until dough is 1/2" below the top of the pan.

6. Move an oven rack to the center of the oven. Preheat oven to 350°F.

7. Remove plastic wrap, slide lid onto pan, and bake for 45 minutes, or until internal temperature reaches 200–205°F.

Tip: If your bread did not rise enough to hit the top of the pan and brown, after baking, you can invert the pan (with the lid on) and bake an additional 10 minutes to brown the top of the loaf.

8. Remove lid, cool slightly in pan, then transfer to a cooling rack to cool completely.

Proofing Time: 4 hours **Bake Time:** 45 minutes **Makes:** One pain de mie

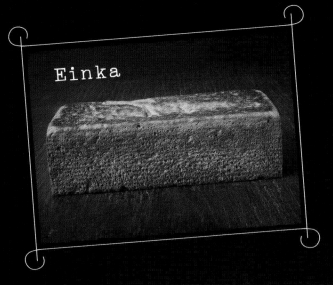

Einka

(continued from p. 118) Speculation varies on exactly why it's called a Pullman loaf, but if you want to stick with a French theme, pain de mie is ideal for making a croque monsieur (pronounced *cock my shoe* with only a hint of the "r")—a toasted sandwich with ham slices between the bread topped with a strong grated cheese like Gruyère on the outside, slightly peppered and salted. The cheese melts and forms a crust. A croque madame has a fried egg on top of the cheese, and a croque mademoiselle is a much lighter vegetarian version using a mild cheese, with a side of salad. As it turns out, the croque idea (based on the verb *croquer*, "to bite") has turned trendy and regional. Now we have croque *señor* (w/salsa), croque *Hawaiian* (w/a slice of pineapple), croque *Norvégien* (w/smoked salmon instead of ham), croque *tartiflette* (w/sliced potatoes and Reblochon cheese), on and on. My version is a little bit of everything, stacked sky high. Croque sky high?

Einkorn

Kamut

Sprouted

Einkorn

It's the night BEFORE Bake Day (p. 58). As usual, you're going to pull 1/2 cup mother from your Refrigerator Mother, feed her 3/8 cup flour and 1/4 cup water, stir/cover, and put her back until next week. To the 1/2 cup mother now in your *Glasslock* bowl that's about to become "activated batter," you'll add 3/8 cup flour and 1/4 cup water; stir/cover.

It's Bake Day. Rise and shine! Feed your activated batter 3/8 cup flour and 1/4 cup water; stir/cover. Two to three hours later, it's ready to go to work for you. This exquisitely flavored soft bread is mixed, shaped, and then refrigerated 12–24 hours. After refrigeration, it's brought back up to room temperature and baked. During its time in the refrigerator, the bread rises a subtle amount. It will also rise ever-so-slightly while it's being brought up to room temperature before baking. The rest of the rise will occur in the oven. Because of the slow nature of the rise, it's important to use a well-seasoned or enameled cast-iron skillet to prevent any discoloration of the loaf from the skillet.

Depending on the type of flour you're using, follow the amounts in the chart below.

	Activated Batter	Water	Olive Oil	Honey	Salt	Flour (same type as mother)	Egg Whites	Sea-Salt Flakes
White	1 1/2 cups	2 cups	2 T	1 T	1 T	6 1/4 cups	1	1 1/4 t
Kamut	1 1/2 cups	2 1/2 cups	2 T	1 T	1 T	6 cups	1	1 1/4 t
Sprouted	1 1/2 cups	2 1/2 cups	2 T	1 T	1 T	7 cups	1	1 1/4 t
Einkorn	1 1/2 cups	2 cups	2 T	1 T	1 T	7 cups	1	1 1/4 t
Einka	1 1/2 cups	2 cups	2 T	1 T	1 T	7 cups	1	1 1/4 t

1. To the batter in your bowl, add water, olive oil, honey, and salt; mix well.

2. Reserve 1 cup flour for kneading and add remaining flour to bowl with batter and mix until a stiff, tacky dough forms. Dust a clean work surface with reserved flour and scoop dough out of bowl. Knead dough until smooth and pliable (about 10 minutes).

3. Generously butter a 12" cast-iron skillet; set aside.

4. Lightly dust a clean work surface with flour and scoop dough from bowl. Divide dough into 4 equal pieces (for good symmetry, weigh using a scale). Shape each piece into an oval. Gently press one end of each oval into a point. Arrange ovals in skillet so the rounded ends touch the sides of the skillet and the pointed ends are in the center of the skillet. Gently press the tips of each oval in the center to fill in any gaps. To sharpen lines between loaves, use a sharp knife to cut along seams.

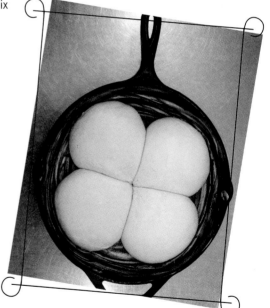

5. Cover skillet with plastic wrap and refrigerate overnight (12 hours) or up to 24 hours.

6. Remove skillet from fridge, remove plastic wrap, cover with a flour-sack cotton towel, and let sit in a warm place (70–73°F) for 2 hours.

7. Preheat oven to 350°F. Using a bread lame, make a 1/4"–1/2"-deep slash down the center of each oval. In a small bowl, combine egg white and 1 t water and mix until frothy. Brush all ovals with egg-white wash and sprinkle with sea-salt flakes. Bake for 45–50 minutes, or until internal temperature reaches 190°F.

For an enticing, open-faced sandwich, cut the top off a whole head of garlic, drizzle with olive oil, wrap in foil, and oven-roast at 400°F for 30 minutes. Cool slightly, then smear a clove onto a toasted slice of Cast-Iron Skillet Bread, add thinly sliced steak and Monterey jack cheese, and broil until the cheese is melted. Top with sautéed oyster mushrooms, fresh watercress, a drizzle of olive oil, fresh rosemary, cracked peppercorns, and sea-salt flakes.

Kamut

White

Einka

Sprouted

Sidewall

Einka

If you'd asked Joseph, he would have told you that rye bread isn't rye bread if it doesn't have chops, slang for cracked rye. For this loaf of rye, you'll need 1 1/2 cups rye flour and 1/2 cup cracked rye (rye chops). Organic heritage dark northern rye flour from BluebirdGrainFarms.com is an heirloom variety that has been passed from farmer to farmer in eastern Washington for over 100 years. They also offer whole rye berries, if you have a way to coarsely crack them. Otherwise, organic cracked rye can be found at BobsRedMill.com or KingArthurFlour.com.

It's the night BEFORE Bake Day (p. 58). As usual, you're going to pull 1/2 cup mother from your Refrigerator Mother, feed her 3/8 cup flour and 1/4 cup water, stir/cover, and put her back until next week. But to make Rustic Rye, this is where your normal routine changes. To the 1/2 cup mother now in your *Glasslock* bowl, you're going to add 1 cup rye flour and 1 cup water (creates approx. 2 1/4 cups activated batter); stir/cover. In addition, you're going to add 1/2 cup cracked rye (rye chops) to a small bowl, fill with water, and cover. Both bowls will rest on your counter overnight (up to 12 hours).

It's Bake Day. Rise and shine!

1. Drain water from cracked rye and add to batter in bowl. Add remaining 1/2 cup rye flour, molasses, honey, caraway, fennel, and salt; mix well.

2. Reserve 1/2 cup flour for kneading. Add remaining flour to bowl with batter and mix until a stiff, tacky dough forms.

Depending on the type of flour you're using, follow the amounts in the chart below.

	Activated Batter	Rye Flour	Molasses	Honey	Caraway (crushed)	Fennel Seed (crushed)	Salt	Flour (same type as mother)	Ice Cubes
White	2 1/4 cups	1 1/2 cups	1 T	2 t	2 t	1/2 t	1 1/2 t	1 1/2 cups	1 cup
Kamut	2 1/4 cups	1 1/2 cups	1 T	2 t	2 t	1/2 t	1 1/2 t	1 1/2 cups	1 cup
Sprouted	2 1/4 cups	1 1/2 cups	1 T	2 t	2 t	1/2 t	1 1/2 t	1 3/4 cups	1 cup
Einkorn	2 1/4 cups	1 1/2 cups	1 T	2 t	2 t	1/2 t	1 1/2 t	1 3/4 cups	1 cup
Einka	2 1/4 cups	1 1/2 cups	1 T	2 t	2 t	1/2 t	1 1/2 t	1 3/4 cups	1 cup

Garlic-Onion Coating

Egg Whites	Poppy Seeds	Sea-Salt Flakes	Sesame Seeds	Garlic Flakes	Onion Flakes
1	3/4 t	1/2 t	1/2 t	1/2 t	1/2 t

3. Dust a clean work surface with reserved flour and scoop dough out of bowl. Knead dough until smooth and pliable (about 5 minutes). Shape dough into a ball.

4. Line an inverted baker's sheet with parchment paper. Place dough on parchment paper and cover with a flour-sack cotton towel. Let rise for 1 1/2 hours.

5. Move an oven rack to the center of the oven and another to the bottom. Place an enameled cast-iron Dutch oven on the bottom rack and a 15"-square baking stone on the center rack. Preheat oven to 425°F.

6. Slide pizza peel under parchment paper and loaf. Using a bread lame, make two swift, superficial cuts into top of loaf to form an "X".

7. Slide bread and parchment paper off pizza peel onto baking stone. Add ice cubes to enameled cast-iron Dutch oven. (Why? See p. 216.) Bake for 20 minutes.

8. Meanwhile, prepare Garlic-Onion Coating: In a small bowl, combine egg white and 1 t water and mix until frothy. In another small bowl, combine poppy seeds, sea-salt flakes, sesame seeds, garlic flakes, and onion flakes. After bread has baked for 20 minutes, remove from oven, using the pizza peel. Brush with egg-white wash and sprinkle with Garlic-Onion Coating. Return to oven and bake an additional 5 minutes, or until internal temperature reaches 190°F.

9. Remove from oven using the pizza peel and transfer to a cooling rack.

100 years later, here we are carving our names into a book

Proofing Time: 1 hour, 30 minutes   Bake Time: 25 minutes   Makes: One 8" loaf

Kamut

To make a classic Reuben sandwich, place two slices of rye bread on a baker's sheet. Layer each slice with Swiss cheese and corned beef. Broil until cheese is melted, then add a heap of sauerkraut (drain it first to keep the sandwich from getting soggy) to one slice. Just before bringing the two slices together, smother one side with this easy Russian dressing: In a small bowl, combine 1/2 cup mayonnaise, 1/4 cup sour cream, 1 T chili sauce, 2 t lemon juice, 1 1/2 t sugar, 1/4 t salt, 1/4 t paprika, and 1/4 t allspice.

Kamut

Sprouted

White

Einkorn

Einka

We all know the true purpose of a hamburger bun—it's for holding all the extras you end up stacking on top of your burger. To that end, a good bun needs to hold up. These do just that, but are still light and fluffy without being heavy or "too much bun." We also know a good hamburger deserves a good side of fries. Who hasn't been served a side of home fries that aren't crisp? My daughter-in-law, Ashley's, version (at right) fixes that problem.

White

It's the night BEFORE Bake Day (p. 58). As usual, you're going to pull 1/2 cup mother from your Refrigerator Mother, feed her 3/8 cup flour and 1/4 cup water, stir/cover, and put her back until next week.

To the 1/2 cup mother now in your *Glasslock* bowl that's about to become "activated batter," you'll add 3/8 cup flour and 1/4 cup water; stir/cover.

It's Bake Day. Rise and shine! Feed your activated batter 3/8 cup flour and 1/4 cup water; stir/cover. Two to three hours later, it's ready to go to work for you.

Depending on the type of flour you're using, follow the amounts in the chart below.

	Activated Batter	Buttermilk	Coconut Oil	Honey	Salt	Flour (same type as mother)	Egg Whites	Sesame Seeds
White	1 1/2 cups	3/4 cup	1/4 cup	1 T	1 1/2 t	2 1/4 cups	1	2 t
Kamut	1 1/2 cups	1 cup	1/4 cup	1 T	1 1/2 t	2 cups	1	2 t
Sprouted	1 1/2 cups	1 cup	1/4 cup	1 T	1 1/2 t	2 cups	1	2 t
Einkorn	1 1/2 cups	3/4 cup	1/4 cup	1 T	1 1/2 t	2 1/2 cups	1	2 t
Einka	1 1/2 cups	3/4 cup	1/4 cup	1 T	1 1/2 t	2 1/4 cups	1	2 t

1. In a small saucepan over low heat, combine buttermilk, coconut oil, honey, and salt. Cook until honey dissolves and coconut oil melts. Using your digital thermometer, test to make sure the mixture isn't hotter than 100°F. Add buttermilk mixture to bowl with batter; mix until smooth.

2. Reserve 1/4 cup flour for kneading. Add remaining flour to bowl with batter and mix until a stiff, tacky dough forms. Dust a clean work surface with reserved flour and scoop dough out of bowl. Knead dough until smooth, pliable, and slightly tacky (about 5 minutes).

3. Wash and dry bowl and coat with coconut oil. Shape dough into a ball and add to bowl. Cover bowl with its lid and let condition in a warm place (70–73°F) for 1 1/2 hours.

4. Preheat oven to 400°F. Line a baker's sheet with parchment paper.

5. Deflate dough and divide into 8 equal portions. Form each portion into a 4 1/2" disk and place on prepared baking sheet. Once all buns are formed, cover with a flour-sack cotton towel and let rise in a warm place (70–73°F) for 30 minutes.

6. After rising (buns will still be a little flat, but will rise more during baking), mix egg white and 1 t water together until frothy. Brush tops of buns with egg-white wash and sprinkle with sesame seeds.

7. Bake for 18–20 minutes, or until golden brown.

CRISP FINGER FRIES

Prep Time: 15 minutes   Cook Time: 50 minutes
Makes: 6 servings

- 2 1/2 lbs red potatoes (about 6 medium potatoes)
- 3 T coconut oil, melted
- 3 garlic cloves, peeled and minced (about 1 T)
- 1/2 t smoked paprika
- 1/2 t salt
- 1/4 t pepper
- fresh minced parsley for garnish (optional)

1. Preheat oven to 450°F. Line a baker's sheet with parchment paper; set aside.
2. Halve potatoes lengthwise and cut into 1/8"- to 1/4"-thick slices. Add potatoes to a large bowl.
3. Add coconut oil, garlic, smoked paprika, salt, and pepper; toss to coat.
4. Bake fries for 25 minutes, stir, and bake an additional 25 minutes or until crisp. If desired, serve with fresh minced parsley.

Proofing Time: 2 hours   Bake Time: 18–20 minutes   Makes: Eight 4 1/2" buns   **131**

PARKER HOUSE ROLLS

White

These richly flavored and decadently buttered dinner rolls originated at the Parker House Hotel (the oldest continuously operating hotel in the U.S.) in Boston, Massachusetts, in the 1800s. Originally made in a pocketbook shape, over the years, home cooks and restaurateurs alike have experimented with shaping techniques to suit their personal tastes. Nowadays, you will find a wide array of options for shaping, including the traditional pocketbook shape, squares, squares split down the center, and even intricate braids. In our recipe, we snugly pack the soft dough into a 9" x 13" baking dish and brush the tops of the rolls with butter before and after baking to create square, high-rising, buttery rolls.

Einka

It's the night BEFORE Bake Day (p. 58). As usual, you're going to pull 1/2 cup mother from your Refrigerator Mother, feed her 3/8 cup flour and 1/4 cup water, stir/cover, and put her back until next week. To the 1/2 cup mother now in your *Glasslock* bowl that's about to become "activated batter," you'll add 3/8 cup flour and 1/4 cup water; stir/cover.

It's Bake Day. Rise and shine! Feed your activated batter 3/8 cup flour and 1/4 cup water; stir/cover. Two to three hours later, it's ready to go to work for you. How about a batch of decadent, melt-in-your-mouth, soft rolls?

Depending on the type of flour you're using, follow the amounts in the chart below.

	Activated Batter	Buttermilk	Butter (divided)	Honey	Salt	Eggs	Flour (same type as mother)
White	1 1/2 cups	1 cup	8 T	2 T	1 1/2 t	2	3 3/4 cups
Kamut	1 1/2 cups	1 1/2 cups	8 T	2 T	1 1/2 t	2	3 1/2 cups
Sprouted	1 1/2 cups	1 1/4 cups	8 T	2 T	1 1/2 t	2	3 3/4 cups
Einkorn	1 1/2 cups	1 cup	8 T	2 T	1 1/2 t	2	4 1/2 cups
Einka	1 1/2 cups	1 cup	8 T	2 T	1 1/2 t	2	4 1/2 cups

1. In a small saucepan over low heat, combine buttermilk, 4 T butter, honey, and salt. Cook until honey dissolves and butter begins to melt. Using your digital thermometer, test to make sure the mixture isn't hotter than 100°F. Add buttermilk mixture and eggs to bowl with batter; mix until smooth.

2. Reserve 1/2 cup flour for kneading. Add remaining flour to bowl with batter and mix until a stiff, tacky dough forms. Dust a clean work surface with reserved flour and scoop dough out of bowl. Knead dough until smooth and pliable (about 5 minutes).

3. Wash and dry bowl and coat with butter. Shape dough into a ball, add to bowl, and cover bowl with its lid. *(Please note: These rolls rise a total of 4 hours before being baked for 35–40 minutes. Should you decide it's a little too early in the day for hot-from-the-oven rolls, you can put the covered dough in the refrigerator up to 4 hours before proceeding with steps 4 through 9.)*

Sprouted

Kamut

4. Let condition in a warm place (70–73°F) for 2 hours.

5. Generously butter a 13" x 9" glass baking dish.

6. Deflate dough and divide into 12 equal portions. Form each portion into a ball and place in prepared baking dish. Once all rolls are formed, cover with a flour-sack cotton towel and let rise for 2 hours in a warm place (70–73°F), or until rolls are level with the top of the baking dish.

7. Preheat oven to 350°F.

8. Melt remaining 4 T butter. Brush tops of rolls with 2 T melted butter.

9. Bake for 35–40 minutes, or until golden brown and internal temperature reaches 200–205°F. Brush tops of rolls with remaining melted butter.

Proofing Time: 4 hours   Bake Time: 35–40 minutes   Makes: Twelve rolls

A precursor to the modern-day pizza, focaccia bread is an Italian flatbread originally baked by ancient Romans on the hearth. (The name comes from the Latin word *focus,* meaning "hearth, place for baking.") Focaccia is traditionally brushed with olive oil during the last rise, which helps preserve moisture, and the signature dimples in the bread act as little wells where the oil and herbs pool into mouth-watering morsels.

(FO cotch ah)
plural: focaccias (FO cotch ahs)

It's the night BEFORE Bake Day (p. 58). As usual, you're going to pull 1/2 cup mother from your Refrigerator Mother, feed her 3/8 cup flour and 1/4 cup water, stir/cover, and put her back until next week.

To the 1/2 cup mother now in your *Glasslock* bowl that's about to become "activated batter," you'll add 3/8 cup flour and 1/4 cup water; stir/cover.

It's Bake Day. Rise and shine! Feed your activated batter 3/8 cup flour and 1/4 cup water; stir/cover. Two to three hours later, it's ready to go to work for you.

Depending on the type of flour you're using, follow the amounts in the chart below.

	Activated Batter	Water	Olive Oil	Honey	Salt	Flour (same type as mother)
White	1 1/2 cups	3/4 cup	2 T	1 T	1 1/2 t	2 1/2 cups
Kamut	1 1/2 cups	1 cup	2 T	1 T	1 1/2 t	2 1/2 cups
Sprouted	1 1/2 cups	1 cup	2 T	1 T	1 1/2 t	3 cups
Einkorn	1 1/2 cups	3/4 cup	2 T	1 T	1 1/2 t	3 cups
Einka	1 1/2 cups	3/4 cup	2 T	1 T	1 1/2 t	3 cups

Toppings

Olive Oil	Oil-Packed Sun-Dried Tomatoes (drained and diced)	Parmesan Cheese (shredded)	Dried Basil	Sea-Salt Flakes	Garlic Flakes
2 T	1/4 cup	1/4 cup	3/4 t	1/2 t	1/4 t

1. To the batter in your bowl, add water, olive oil, honey, and salt; mix well.

2. Reserve 1/2 cup flour for kneading. Add remaining flour to bowl with batter and mix until a stiff, tacky dough forms. Dust a clean work surface with reserved flour and scoop dough out of bowl. Knead dough until smooth and pliable (about 5 minutes).

3. Wash and dry bowl and coat with olive oil. Shape dough into a ball and add to bowl. Cover bowl with its lid and let condition in a warm place (70–73°F) for 2 hours.

4. Lightly oil a baker's sheet with olive oil and line with a sheet of parchment paper.

5. Scoop dough out of bowl onto prepared baker's sheet. With lightly oiled hands, press dough flat so that it covers the entire surface of the baker's sheet, leaving little dimples in the dough as you work.

Sprouted

6. Brush top of dough with olive oil and sprinkle tomatoes, cheese, basil, sea-salt flakes, and garlic flakes over dough. Cover with plastic wrap and let rise in a warm place (70–73°F) for 30 minutes.

7. Move an oven rack to the center of the oven. Place a 15"-square baking stone on the center rack. Preheat oven to 375°F.

8. Remove plastic wrap, place baking sheet on baking stone, and bake for 25 minutes, or until edges are golden brown and internal temperature reaches 190°F.

Proofing Time: 2 hours, 30 minutes   Bake Time: 25 minutes   Makes: One focaccia   **135**

Brown Rice

White Rice

Quinoa

It's the night BEFORE Bake Day (p. 58). As usual, you're going to pull 1/2 cup mother from your Refrigerator Mother, feed her 3/8 cup flour and 1/4 cup water, stir/cover, and put her back until next week.

To the 1/2 cup mother now in your *Glasslock* bowl that's about to become "activated batter," you'll add 3/8 cup flour and 1/4 cup water; stir/cover.

It's Bake Day. Rise and shine! Feed your activated batter 3/8 cup flour and 1/4 cup water; stir/cover. Two to three hours later, it's ready to go to work for you.

Depending on the type of flour you're using, follow the amounts in the chart below.

	Activated Batter	Water	Olive Oil	Honey	Salt	Flour (same type as mother)	B.F.M. Rice Starch*
White Rice	1 1/2 cups	3 cups	2 T	1 T	1 1/2 t	2 cups	3/4 cup
Brown Rice	1 1/2 cups	2 1/2 cups	2 T	1 T	1 1/2 t	2 1/2 cups	1 cup
Quinoa	1 1/2 cups	1 1/2 cups	2 T	1 T	1 1/2 t	4 cups	none

*Barron Flour Mill rice starch, p. 195

Toppings

Olive Oil	Oil-Packed Sun-Dried Tomatoes (drained and diced)	Parmesan Cheese (shredded)	Dried Basil	Sea-Salt Flakes	Garlic Flakes
2 T	1/4 cup	1/4 cup	3/4 t	1/2 t	1/4 t

1. To the batter in your bowl, add water, olive oil, honey, and salt; mix well.

2. Add about half the required flour (and the rice starch, if using). Mix until a tacky dough forms; let rest 5 minutes.

3. Mix in remaining flour.

4. Cover bowl with its lid, and let condition in a warm place (70–73°F) for 2 hours.

5. Lightly oil a baker's sheet with olive oil and line with a sheet of parchment paper.

White Rice

6. Scoop dough out of bowl onto prepared baker's sheet (dough will be very wet and almost like a batter). Using a spatula, spread dough out so that it covers the entire surface of the baker's sheet.

7. Sprinkle olive oil, tomatoes, cheese, dried basil, sea-salt flakes, and garlic flakes over dough. Cover with plastic wrap and let rise in a warm place (70–73°F) for 30 minutes.

8. Move an oven rack to the center of the oven. Place a 15"-square baking stone on the center rack. Preheat oven to 375°F.

9. Remove plastic wrap, place baking sheet on baking stone, and bake for 25 minutes, or until edges are golden brown and internal temperature reaches 190°F.

BRAIDED BREADSTICKS

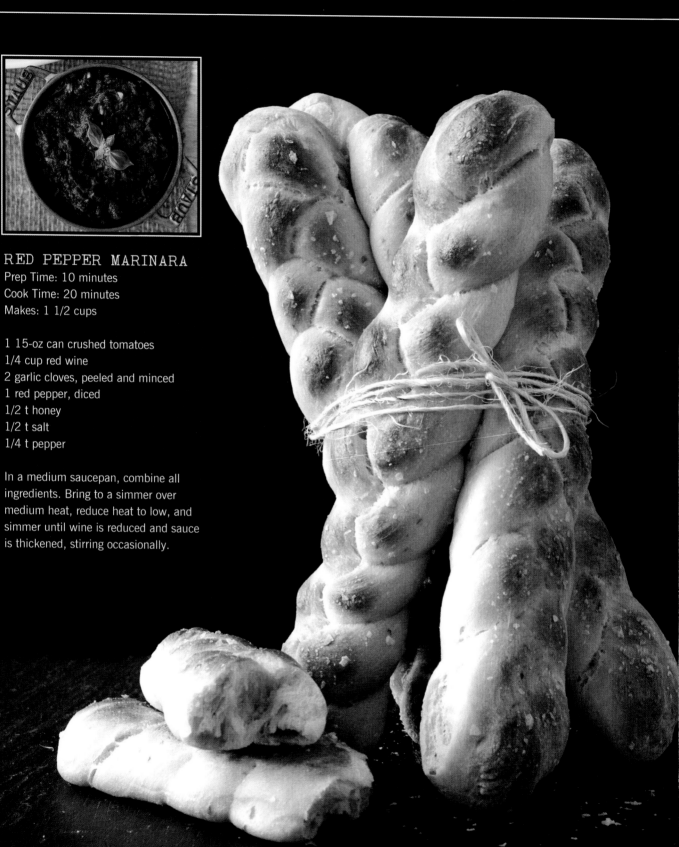

RED PEPPER MARINARA
Prep Time: 10 minutes
Cook Time: 20 minutes
Makes: 1 1/2 cups

1 15-oz can crushed tomatoes
1/4 cup red wine
2 garlic cloves, peeled and minced
1 red pepper, diced
1/2 t honey
1/2 t salt
1/4 t pepper

In a medium saucepan, combine all ingredients. Bring to a simmer over medium heat, reduce heat to low, and simmer until wine is reduced and sauce is thickened, stirring occasionally.

It's the night BEFORE Bake Day (p. 58). As usual, you're going to pull 1/2 cup mother from your Refrigerator Mother, feed her 3/8 cup flour and 1/4 cup water, stir/cover, and put her back until next week.

To the 1/2 cup mother now in your *Glasslock* bowl that's about to become "activated batter," you'll add 3/8 cup flour and 1/4 cup water; stir/cover.

It's Bake Day. Rise and shine! Feed your activated batter 3/8 cup flour and 1/4 cup water; stir/cover. Two to three hours later, it's ready to go to work for you.

Depending on the type of flour you're using, follow the amounts in the chart below.

	Activated Batter	Water	Semolina Flour	Salt	Fresh Rosemary (minced)	Honey	Flour (same type as mother)	Egg Whites	Sea-Salt Flakes
White	1 1/2 cups	1 1/2 cups	2 T	1 1/2 t	1 1/2 t	1 t	4 cups	1	1/2 t
Kamut	1 1/2 cups	1 1/2 cups	2 T	1 1/2 t	1 1/2 t	1 t	2 3/4 cups	1	1/2 t
Sprouted	1 1/2 cups	1 1/2 cups	2 T	1 1/2 t	1 1/2 t	1 t	3 3/4 cups	1	1/2 t
Einkorn	1 1/2 cups	1 1/2 cups	2 T	1 1/2 t	1 1/2 t	1 t	5 cups	1	1/2 t
Einka	1 1/2 cups	1 1/2 cups	2 T	1 1/2 t	1 1/2 t	1 t	4 1/4 cups	1	1/2 t

1. To the batter in your bowl, add water, semolina, salt, rosemary, and honey; mix well.

2. Reserve 1/2 cup flour for kneading. Add remaining flour to bowl with batter and mix until a stiff, tacky dough forms. Dust a clean work surface with reserved flour and scoop dough out of bowl. Knead dough until smooth and pliable (about 5 minutes).

3. Wash and dry bowl and coat with safflower oil. Shape dough into a ball and add to bowl. Cover bowl with its lid and let condition in a warm place (70–73°F) for 2 hours.

4. Preheat oven to 400°F and line two baker's sheets with parchment paper.

5. Deflate dough and divide it into 30 equal portions, dusting with flour as needed.

6. Roll each piece into a rope roughly 11" long. Join 3 ropes together at one end and braid, securing at the other end. Repeat with remaining ropes to make a total of 10 braids.

7. Transfer braids to prepared baking sheets, cover each with a flour-sack cotton towel, and let rise for 30 minutes.

8. In a small bowl, combine egg white and 1 t water and mix until frothy. Brush over braids and sprinkle with sea-salt flakes. Bake for 20 minutes, rotating baking sheets halfway through, until breadsticks are light-golden brown and internal temperature reaches 190°F.

Kamut

Proofing Time: 2 hours, 30 minutes **Bake Time:** 20 minutes **Makes:** Ten breadsticks

Sprouted

It's the night BEFORE Bake Day (p. 58). As usual, you're going to pull 1/2 cup mother from your Refrigerator Mother, feed her 3/8 cup flour and 1/4 cup water, stir/cover, and put her back until next week.

To the 1/2 cup mother now in your *Glasslock* bowl that's about to become "activated batter," you'll add 3/8 cup flour and 1/4 cup water; stir/cover.

It's Bake Day. Rise and shine! Feed your activated batter 3/8 cup flour and 1/4 cup water; stir/cover. Two to three hours later, it's ready to go to work for you.

Depending on the type of flour you're using, follow the amounts in the chart below.

	Activated Batter	Water	Semolina Flour	Salt	Honey	Flour (same type as mother)	Egg Whites
White	1 1/2 cups	1 1/2 cups	2 T	1 1/2 t	1 t	4 cups	1
Kamut	1 1/2 cups	1 1/2 cups	2 T	1 1/2 t	1 t	2 3/4 cups	1
Sprouted	1 1/2 cups	1 1/2 cups	2 T	1 1/2 t	1 t	3 3/4 cups	1
Einkorn	1 1/2 cups	1 1/2 cups	2 T	1 1/2 t	1 t	5 cups	1
Einka	1 1/2 cups	1 1/2 cups	2 T	1 1/2 t	1 t	4 1/4 cups	1

1. To the batter in your bowl, add water, semolina, salt, and honey; mix well.

2. Reserve 1/2 cup flour for kneading. Add remaining flour to bowl with batter and mix until a stiff, tacky dough forms. Dust a clean work surface with reserved flour and scoop dough out of bowl. Knead dough until smooth and pliable (about 5 minutes).

3. Wash and dry bowl and coat with safflower oil. Shape dough into a ball and add to bowl. Cover bowl with its lid and let condition in a warm place (70–73°F) for 2 hours.

4. Preheat oven to 450°F. Line two baker's sheets with parchment paper.

5. Add 8 cups of water to a 3.5-qt saucepan and bring to a boil.

6. Deflate dough and divide it into 12 equal portions (if dough is sticky, lightly dust with flour). Roll each portion into a ball, and then make a hole in the center of each bagel with your fingers and stretch the bagel out into an even ring.

7. Place bagels into the saucepan, leaving enough room for each bagel to expand without being crowded (1–3 at a time). Boil for 2 minutes, then flip over with a stainless-steel skimmer and boil for an additional 2 minutes. Transfer bagels to prepared baking sheets and repeat this process with remaining bagels.

8. In a small bowl, combine egg white and 1 t water and mix until frothy; brush over boiled bagels. Bake for 25 minutes, rotating baking sheets halfway through, until bagels are light-golden brown and internal temperature reaches 190°F.

Einka

Einka

Kamut

Einkorn/Einka
p. 193

143

Kamut

White

It's the night BEFORE Bake Day (p. 58). As usual, you're going to pull 1/2 cup mother from your Refrigerator Mother, feed her 3/8 cup flour and 1/4 cup water, stir/cover, and put her back until next week.

To the 1/2 cup mother now in your *Glasslock* bowl that's about to become "activated batter," you'll add 3/8 cup flour and 1/4 cup water; stir/cover.

It's Bake Day. Rise and shine! Feed your activated batter 3/8 cup flour and 1/4 cup water; stir/cover. Two to three hours later, it's ready to go to work for you.

Depending on the type of flour you're using, follow the amounts in the chart below.

	Activated Batter	Water	Salt	Honey	Flour (same type as mother)	Baking Soda	Sea-Salt Flakes	Butter
White	1 1/2 cups	1 1/2 cups	1 1/2 t	1 t	4 1/4 cups	1/3 cup	1 t	2 T
Kamut	1 1/2 cups	1 1/2 cups	1 1/2 t	1 t	3 1/4 cups	1/3 cup	1 t	2 T
Sprouted	1 1/2 cups	1 1/2 cups	1 1/2 t	1 t	4 cups	1/3 cup	1 t	2 T
Einkorn	1 1/2 cups	1 1/2 cups	1 1/2 t	1 t	5 1/2 cups	1/3 cup	1 t	2 T
Einka	1 1/2 cups	1 1/2 cups	1 1/2 t	1 t	4 1/4 cups	1/3 cup	1 t	2 T

1. To the batter in your bowl, add water, salt, and honey; mix well.

2. Reserve 1/2 cup flour for kneading. Add remaining flour to bowl with batter and mix until a stiff, tacky dough forms. Dust a clean work surface with reserved flour and scoop dough out of bowl. Knead dough until smooth and pliable (about 5 minutes).

3. Wash and dry bowl and coat with safflower oil. Shape dough into a ball and add to bowl. Cover bowl with its lid and let condition in a warm place (70–73°F) for 2 hours.

4. Preheat oven to 425°F. Line two baker's sheets with parchment paper.

5. Add 8 cups of water to a 3.5-qt saucepan and bring to a boil.

6. Deflate dough and divide into 8 equal portions. Roll each portion into a 24"-long rope, dusting with flour as needed. Working with one rope at a time, shape into a U, twist the ends, bring ends to the bottom of the U, and attach an end to each side of the U, gently pressing to secure. Complete process with remaining ropes.

7. Dissolve baking soda in boiling water. Working in batches so the pretzels don't get crowded in the saucepan, boil pretzels for 1–2 minutes, or until they puff up and float to the surface. Remove pretzels from pot using a stainless-steel skimmer. Transfer to prepared baking sheets, sprinkle with sea-salt flakes, and bake for 16–18 minutes, rotating baking sheets halfway through, until deep-golden brown and internal temperature reaches 190°F.

8. Melt butter and brush over pretzels.

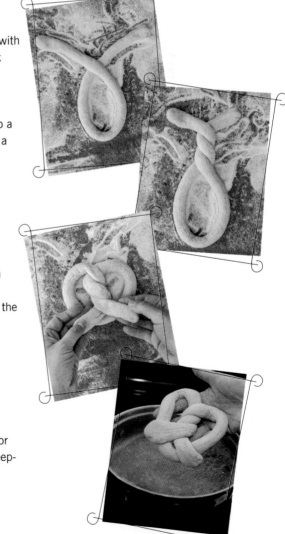

Before you get to thinking a bialy is just a bagel with onions in the middle, consider this: Bagels are boiled before baking and have a hole in the center. Bialys go straight into the oven and there's a depression in the center, not a hole. A Yiddish dish originating in Bialystock, Poland, which was made famous because of the musical *Fiddler on the Roof*, bialys are in a class all their own. I like to eat them either plain or toasted, with butter or cream cheese. Smoked fish or a slice of turkey with mustard on top turns a bialy into a meal for me. A bialy combines the texture of an English muffin with the heft and chew of a bagel. If you've never tasted a bialy, it's time to show it some love.

(be AL ley)

plural: bialys (bee AL leys)

Sprouted

Joseph told me that he used to rub an onion cut in half on the windshields of his vehicles to keep snow from sticking.

Einka

Einkorn

146

It's the night BEFORE Bake Day (p. 58). As usual, you're going to pull 1/2 cup mother from your Refrigerator Mother, feed her 3/8 cup flour and 1/4 cup water, stir/cover, and put her back until next week.

To the 1/2 cup mother now in your *Glasslock* bowl that's about to become "activated batter," you'll add 3/8 cup flour and 1/4 cup water; stir/cover.

It's Bake Day. Rise and shine! Feed your activated batter 3/8 cup flour and 1/4 cup water; stir/cover. Two to three hours later, it's ready to go to work for you.

Depending on the type of flour you're using, follow the amounts in the chart below.

	Activated Batter	Water	Salt	Honey	Flour (same type as mother)
White	1 1/2 cups	1 1/2 cups	1 1/2 t	1 t	4 1/4 cups
Kamut	1 1/2 cups	1 1/2 cups	1 1/2 t	1 t	3 1/4 cups
Sprouted	1 1/2 cups	1 1/2 cups	1 1/2 t	1 t	4 cups
Einkorn	1 1/2 cups	1 1/2 cups	1 1/2 t	1 t	5 1/2 cups
Einka	1 1/2 cups	1 1/2 cups	1 1/2 t	1 t	4 1/2 cups

Onion Filling

Yellow Onion (peeled and minced)	Safflower Oil	Poppy Seeds	Salt
2 cups	1 T	1/2 t	1/4 t

1. To the batter in your bowl, add water, salt, and honey; mix well.

2. Reserve 1/2 cup flour for kneading. Add remaining flour to bowl with batter and mix until a stiff, tacky dough forms. Dust a clean work surface with reserved flour and scoop dough out of bowl. Knead dough until smooth and pliable (about 5 minutes).

3. Wash and dry bowl and coat with safflower oil. Shape dough into a ball and add to bowl. Cover bowl with its lid and let condition in a warm place (70–73°F) for 2 hours.

4. Prepare Onion Filling: Add minced onions and safflower oil to a large skillet and cook over medium-low heat until onions are soft, stirring occasionally. Remove from heat. Mix in poppy seeds and salt; set aside.

5. Preheat oven to 450°F. Line two inverted baker's sheets with parchment paper. Place a 15"-square baking stone on the center oven rack.

6. Deflate dough and divide it into 12 equal portions (if dough is sticky, lightly dust with flour). Roll each portion into a ball, flatten each ball slightly, and make a depression in the center to hold the filling. Place dough on parchment paper (6 bialys to each baking sheet). Evenly divide filling between depressions. Cover with a flour-sack cotton towel and let rise for 30 minutes.

7. Slide pizza peel under parchment paper and bialys. Slide bialys and parchment paper off pizza peel onto baking stone.

8. Bake bialys, 6 at a time, for 20 minutes, or until bialys are light-golden brown and internal temperature reaches 190°F.

STROMBOLI

Stromboli is basically a pizza rolled into a log and baked to bubbly, golden-brown perfection. Two restaurateurs, one in nearby Spokane, Washington, claim to have first invented the Stromboli (named after an Italian movie) in the 1950s. Strombolis can be made with any of your favorite pizza or sandwich ingredients; simply roll out, top, roll up, and bake, then slice into pretty pinwheels to serve.

(STROM buh lee)
plural: Strombolis (STROM buh lees)

148

Einka

It's the night BEFORE Bake Day (p. 58). As usual, you're going to pull 1/2 cup mother from your Refrigerator Mother, feed her 3/8 cup flour and 1/4 cup water, stir/cover, and put her back until next week.

To the 1/2 cup mother now in your *Glasslock* bowl that's about to become "activated batter," you'll add 3/8 cup flour and 1/4 cup water; stir/cover.

It's Bake Day. Rise and shine! Feed your activated batter 3/8 cup flour and 1/4 cup water; stir/cover. Two to three hours later, it's ready to go to work for you.

Depending on the type of flour you're using, follow the amounts in the chart below.

	Activated Batter	Water	Olive Oil	Salt	Honey	Flour (same type as mother)	Egg Whites
White	1 1/2 cups	1/2 cup	1 T	1 t	1 t	2 1/2 cups	1
Kamut	1 1/2 cups	1/2 cup	1 T	1 t	1 t	1 1/2 cups	1
Sprouted	1 1/2 cups	1/2 cup	1 T	1 t	1 t	2 1/4 cups	1
Einkorn	1 1/2 cups	1/2 cup	1 T	1 t	1 t	3 cups	1
Einka	1 1/2 cups	1/2 cup	1 T	1 t	1 t	2 1/2 cups	1

Stromboli Filling

Mozzarella Cheese (shredded)	Marinated Artichoke Hearts (drained)	Pepperoni (drained)	Salami (sliced)	Sliced Olives (drained)	Feta Cheese (crumbled)
2 cups	1/2 cup	6 ozs	2 ozs	1/2 cup	1/4 cup

1. To the batter in your bowl, add water, olive oil, salt, and honey; mix well.

2. Reserve 1/2 cup flour for kneading. Add remaining flour to bowl with mother and mix until a stiff, tacky dough forms. Dust a clean work surface with reserved flour and scoop dough out of bowl. Knead dough until smooth and pliable (about 5 minutes).

3. Wash and dry bowl and coat with olive oil. Shape dough into a ball and add to bowl. Cover bowl with its lid and refrigerate until ready to use (up to 12 hours). When you are ready to make Stromboli, remove dough from refrigerator.

4. Line a baker's sheet with parchment paper. Dust a clean work surface with flour and scoop dough out of bowl. Roll dough out to a 16" x 18" rectangle.

5. Add Stromboli Filling: Spread mozzarella over the dough, leaving about 1 1/2" of space on all four sides. Add artichoke hearts, pepperoni, salami, olives, and feta. Starting from the 16" side, begin rolling dough (just as if you were making cinnamon rolls). When you reach the other 16" side, pinch the bottom seam closed. Tuck ends of the loaf under and pinch seams to seal.

6. Transfer loaf to prepared baker's sheet, cover with a flour-sack cotton towel, and let rise for 30 minutes.

7. Preheat oven to 425°F. Bake Stromboli for 40 minutes, covering with foil halfway through to prevent over-browning.

8. Meanwhile, in a small bowl, combine egg white and 1 t water and mix until frothy. After Stromboli has baked for 40 minutes, remove foil, brush with egg-white wash, and bake an additional 5–10 minutes, or until internal temperature reaches 200–205°F.

CALZONES

These Italian treats have all the mouthwatering goodness of a pizza in a handy, portable package. We love the savory combination of pesto, chicken, bacon, spinach, and of course, mozzarella in this recipe. The dough bakes up to soft-yet-crisp perfection. If you're craving plain ole pizza, whip up a batch of calzone crust, roll it out to a 15" circle, transfer it to a 14" pizza pan lined with parchment paper, shape the edges, and poke a few holes in the crust to prevent air bubbles. Bake in a preheated 425°F oven for 10 minutes. Add your favorite toppings, and bake another 10–15 minutes, or until cheese is melted and bubbling.

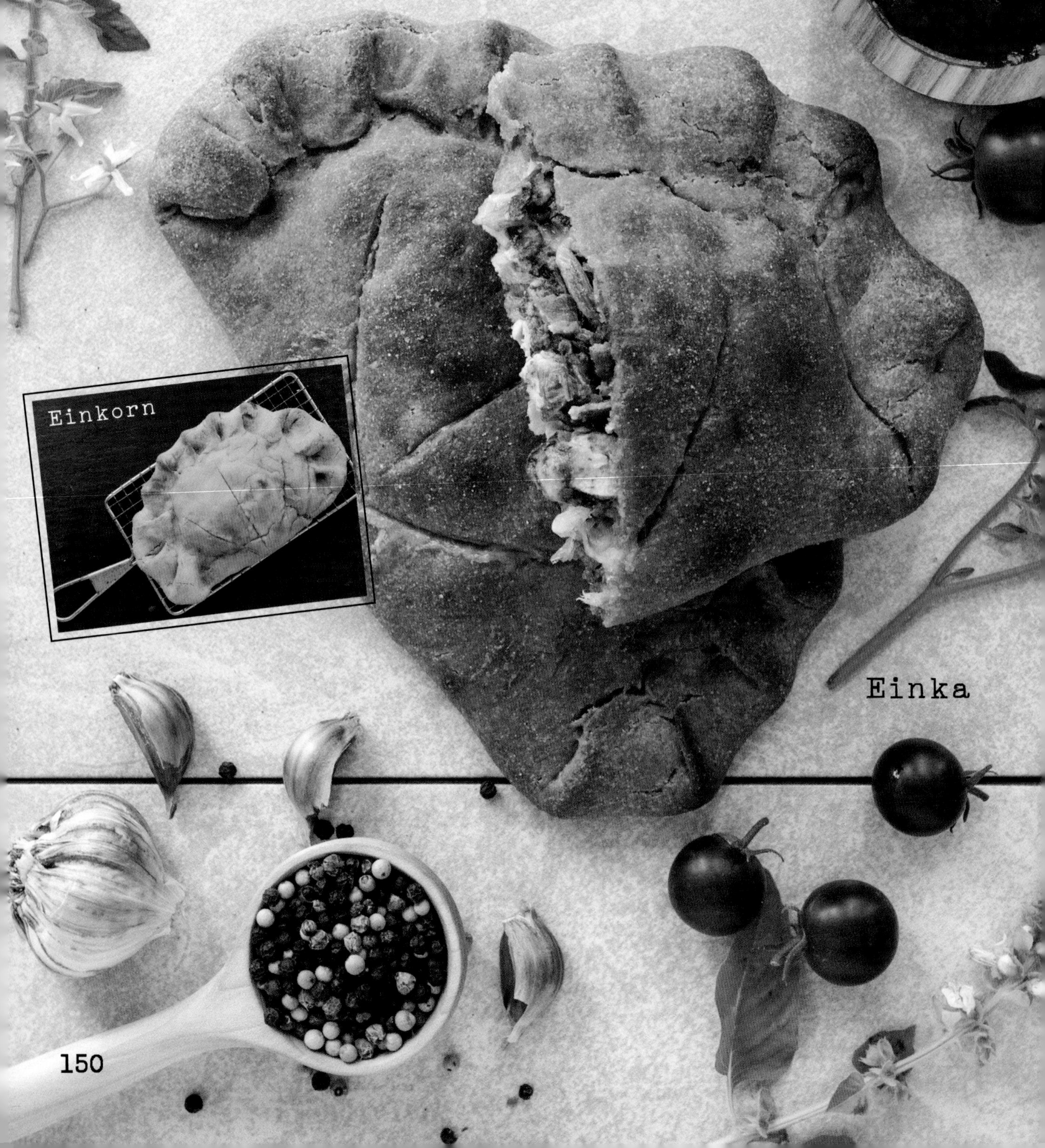

Einkorn

Einka

It's the night BEFORE Bake Day (p. 58). As usual, you're going to pull 1/2 cup mother from your Refrigerator Mother, feed her 3/8 cup flour and 1/4 cup water, stir/cover, and put her back until next week.

To the 1/2 cup mother now in your *Glasslock* bowl that's about to become "activated batter," you'll add 3/8 cup flour and 1/4 cup water; stir/cover.

It's Bake Day. Rise and shine! Feed your activated batter 3/8 cup flour and 1/4 cup water; stir/cover. Two to three hours later, it's ready to go to work for you.

Depending on the type of flour you're using, follow the amounts in the chart below.

	Activated Batter	Semolina Flour	Safflower Oil	Honey	Salt	Flour (same type as mother)
White	1 1/2 cups	2 T	1 1/2 t	1/2 t	1/4 t	1 1/4 cups
Kamut	1 1/2 cups	2 T	1 1/2 t	1/2 t	1/4 t	3/4 cup
Sprouted	1 1/2 cups	2 T	1 1/2 t	1/2 t	1/4 t	1 cup
Einkorn	1 1/2 cups	2 T	1 1/2 t	1/2 t	1/4 t	1 1/2 cups
Einka	1 1/2 cups	2 T	1 1/2 t	1/2 t	1/4 t	1 1/4 cups

Calzone Filling

Chicken Breast (cooked, diced, and divided)	Pesto (divided)	Mozzarella Cheese (shredded and divided)	Frozen Spinach (thawed, squeezed dry, and divided)	Bacon (cooked and diced)	Safflower Oil
8 ozs	8 t	1 cup	4 ozs	4 ozs	2 t

1. To the batter in your bowl, add semolina, safflower oil, honey, and salt; mix well.

2. Reserve 1/4 cup flour for kneading. Add remaining flour to bowl with mother and mix until a stiff, tacky dough forms. Dust a clean work surface with reserved flour and scoop dough out of bowl. Knead dough until smooth and pliable (about 5 minutes).

3. Wash and dry bowl and coat with safflower oil. Shape dough into a ball and add to bowl. Cover bowl with its lid and refrigerate until ready to use (up to 12 hours). When you are ready to make calzones, remove dough from refrigerator.

4. Line an inverted baker's sheet with parchment paper. Dust a clean work surface with flour and scoop dough out of bowl. Divide dough into 2 equal portions. Roll one portion out to a 9 1/2" circle and transfer to prepared baker's sheet.

5. Add Calzone Filling: Add half of chicken to one side of circle, leaving 1" of space along the outer edge. Add 2 t pesto, 1/4 cup mozzarella cheese, half of the spinach and bacon, another 2 t pesto, and another 1/4 cup mozzarella cheese. Fold dough over filling and press edges to seal. Create a decorative edge by folding and twisting the outer edge in toward the calzone. Repeat process with second half of dough. Cover with a flour-sack cotton towel and let rise for 30 minutes.

6. Before bread finishes its 30-minute rise, move an oven rack to the center of the oven. Place a 15"-square baking stone on the center rack. Preheat oven to 425°F.

7. Using a bread lame, make 3–4 cuts in tops of calzones to vent. Brush top of each calzone with 1 t safflower oil.

8. Lift center of parchment paper and fold to create a pleat so both calzones will fit on pizza peel at once. Slide pizza peel under parchment paper and calzones. Slide calzones and parchment paper off pizza peel onto baking stone. Bake for 25 minutes, or until crust is golden brown.

White

It's the night BEFORE Bake Day (p. 58). As usual, you're going to pull 1/2 cup mother from your Refrigerator Mother, feed her 3/8 cup flour and 1/4 cup water, stir/cover, and put her back until next week.

To the 1/2 cup mother now in your *Glasslock* bowl that's about to become "activated batter," you'll add 3/8 cup flour and 1/4 cup water; stir/cover.

It's Bake Day. Rise and shine! Feed your activated batter 3/8 cup flour and 1/4 cup water; stir/cover. Two to three hours later, it's ready to go to work for you.

Depending on the type of flour you're using, follow the amounts in the chart below.

	Activated Batter	Water	Olive Oil (divided)	Salt	Honey	Flour (same type as mother)
White	1 1/2 cups	1/2 cup	4 T	1 t	1 t	2 1/2 cups
Kamut	1 1/2 cups	1/2 cup	4 T	1 t	1 t	1 1/2 cups
Sprouted	1 1/2 cups	1/2 cup	4 T	1 t	1 t	2 1/4 cups
Einkorn	1 1/2 cups	1/2 cup	4 T	1 t	1 t	3 cups
Einka	1 1/2 cups	1/2 cup	4 T	1 t	1 t	2 1/2 cups

1. To the batter in your bowl, add water, 1 T olive oil, salt, and honey; mix well.

2. Reserve 1/2 cup flour for kneading. Add remaining flour to bowl with batter and mix until a stiff, tacky dough forms. Dust a clean work surface with reserved flour and scoop dough out of bowl. Knead dough until smooth and pliable (about 5 minutes).

3. Wash and dry bowl and coat with olive oil. Shape dough into a ball and add to bowl. Cover bowl with its lid and let condition in a warm place (70–73°F) for 2 hours.

4. Preheat oven to 400°F. Generously brush two baker's sheets with olive oil (about 1 1/2 t for each sheet).

5. Lightly dust a clean work surface with flour. Deflate dough and divide into 8 equal portions. Roll each portion into an 8" circle. Place two circles onto each prepared baker's sheet (since only two will fit on a baker's sheet at once, you'll only bake four at a time).

6. Lightly brush tops with 3/4 t olive oil and bake for 4 minutes. Remove from oven. Flip flatbreads over, rotate baking sheets, and bake an additional 6 minutes, or until flatbreads are light-golden brown in spots. Transfer to a cooling rack to cool completely and repeat with remaining flatbread circles.

Kamut

Einkorn

Proofing Time: 2 hours **Bake Time:** 20 minutes **Makes:** Eight 8" flatbreads

BRIOCHE

A brioche is a slightly sweet, rich loaf of French origin, traditionally served for breakfast or, with the addition of fruit, for dessert. As with many breads, brioches can be made in an array of shapes and sizes. One of the traditional shapes is *brioche à tête*. (Literally, "brioche with head.") This classic shape is achieved by placing a large ball of dough into a small, fluted, flared tin and topping it with a second, smaller ball of dough. Another version—the one we chose for this recipe—is a loaf achieved by arranging balls of dough in rows in a loaf pan, which results in a "bubbly" top. In any form, the surface of a brioche has a deep, golden color with a rich sheen.

(BREE ohsh)
plural: brioches (BREE ohsh ez)

White

It's the night BEFORE Bake Day (p. 58). As usual, you're going to pull 1/2 cup mother from your Refrigerator Mother, feed her 3/8 cup flour and 1/4 cup water, stir/cover, and put her back until next week.

To the 1/2 cup mother now in your *Glasslock* bowl that's about to become "activated batter," you'll add 3/8 cup flour and 1/4 cup water; stir/cover.

It's Bake Day. Rise and shine! Feed your activated batter 3/8 cup flour and 1/4 cup water; stir/cover. Two to three hours later, it's ready to go to work for you.

Depending on the type of flour you're using, follow the amounts in the chart below.

	Activated Batter	Buttermilk	Honey	Eggs (separated)	Salt	Flour (same type as mother)	Butter (softened)
White	1 1/2 cups	1 cup	1/4 cup	3	1 t	4 1/2 cups	8 T
Kamut	1 1/2 cups	1 cup	1/4 cup	3	1 t	3 3/4 cups	8 T
Sprouted	1 1/2 cups	1 cup	1/4 cup	3	1 t	4 cups	8 T
Einkorn	1 1/2 cups	1 cup	1/4 cup	3	1 t	5 1/2 cups	8 T
Einka	1 1/2 cups	1 cup	1/4 cup	3	1 t	4 1/2 cups	8 T

1. To the batter in your bowl, add buttermilk, honey, 2 whole eggs and 1 egg yolk (reserve white for egg-white wash), and salt; mix well.

2. In another large bowl or a stand mixer fitted with a dough hook, add flour. Make a well in the center of the flour to receive the liquid and add wet ingredients. Mix until a stiff, tacky dough forms.

3. Cut butter into pieces. With mixer running or by hand, add butter, one piece at a time. Continue to mix until butter is incorporated into dough.

4. Wash and dry *Glasslock* bowl and coat with butter. Lightly dust a clean work surface with flour and scoop dough from bowl or stand mixer. Shape dough into a ball and add to buttered bowl. Cover bowl with its lid and let condition in a warm place (70–73°F) for 2 hours.

Sprouted

5. Generously butter two *Norpro* 8"L x 4.5"W x 3"H nonstick pans.

6. Deflate dough and divide into 32 equal pieces. Shape each piece into a ball. Place a layer of 8 balls into the bottom of each loaf pan. Add a second layer of 8 balls to each pan, resting them on the sides of the pan. Cover with plastic wrap and let rise in a warm place for 2 hours, or until dough is level with the top of the pan.

7. Make egg-white wash: In a small bowl, combine reserved egg white and 1 t water. Mix until frothy and strain mixture through a fine-mesh sieve to remove clumps (this creates a smooth, glossy finish on brioche).

8. Preheat oven to 350°F.

9. Place loaves on a baking sheet, remove plastic wrap, brush tops with egg-white wash, and bake for 30 minutes, covering with foil halfway through to prevent over-browning. Remove from oven, brush with egg-white wash again, and bake an additional 10 minutes, or until tops are deep-golden brown and internal temperature reaches 200–205°F.

Proofing Time: 4 hours   Bake Time: 40 minutes   Makes: Two 8" brioches

Kamut

(BAR ah BRITH)
plural: baras brith (BAR ahs BRITH)

Bara brith ("speckled bread" in Welsh) is a teabread studded with dried fruits and spices. The term has lent itself to a popular British colloquialism: to "over-spice the bara brith" means to do something in excess. Traditionally, the dried fruits are softened by soaking overnight in black tea. The tea, along with ginger, orange zest, cinnamon, nutmeg, and cloves meld wonderfully and add incredible depth of flavor to the bread. The texture of the bread is moist, with a slight chew that incites dreams of toast, butter, preserves, and a piping-hot cup of tea.

It's the night BEFORE Bake Day (p. 58). As usual, you're going to pull 1/2 cup mother from your Refrigerator Mother, feed her 3/8 cup flour and 1/4 cup water, stir/cover, and put her back until next week.

To the 1/2 cup mother now in your *Glasslock* bowl that's about to become "activated batter," you'll add 3/8 cup flour and 1/4 cup water; stir/cover.

You'll also need to soak the dried fruit for this recipe. To do this, combine the ingredients listed in the chart below in a medium bowl, cover with plastic wrap, and refrigerate overnight.

Black Tea (brewed)	Honey	Raisins	Golden Raisins	Currants	Crystallized Ginger (diced)
2 cups	2 T	1/3 cup	1/3 cup	1/3 cup	1 T

It's Bake Day. Rise and shine! Feed your activated batter 3/8 cup flour and 1/4 cup water; stir/cover. Two to three hours later, it's ready to go to work for you.

Depending on the type of flour you're using, follow the amounts in the chart below.

	Activated Batter	Brown Sugar	Eggs	Orange Zest	Salt	Cinnamon	Nutmeg (ground)	Cloves (ground)	Flour (same type as mother)
White	1 1/2 cups	1/4 cup	1	1 T	1 t	1 t	1/2 t	1/8 t	4 1/2 cups
Kamut	1 1/2 cups	1/4 cup	1	1 T	1 t	1 t	1/2 t	1/8 t	4 cups
Sprouted	1 1/2 cups	1/4 cup	1	1 T	1 t	1 t	1/2 t	1/8 t	4 cups
Einkorn	1 1/2 cups	1/4 cup	1	1 T	1 t	1 t	1/2 t	1/8 t	6 1/2 cups
Einka	1 1/2 cups	1/4 cup	1	1 T	1 t	1 t	1/2 t	1/8 t	4 1/2 cups

1. To the batter in your bowl, add dried fruit mixture (including the tea it was soaked in), brown sugar, egg, orange zest, salt, cinnamon, nutmeg, and cloves; mix well.

2. Reserve 1/2 cup flour for kneading. Add remaining flour to bowl with batter and mix until a stiff, tacky dough forms. Dust a clean work surface with reserved flour and scoop dough out of bowl. Knead dough until smooth and pliable (about 5 minutes).

3. Wash and dry bowl and coat with butter. Shape dough into a ball and add to bowl. Cover bowl with its lid and let condition in a warm place (70–73°F) for 2 hours.

White

4. Generously butter two *Norpro* 8"L x 4.5"W x 3"H nonstick pans.

5. Deflate dough and divide into 2 equal pieces. Shape each piece into an oval, and add an oval to each prepared pan. Cover with plastic wrap and let rise in a warm place (70–73°F) for 3 hours, or until dough is level with the top of the pan.

6. Preheat oven to 350°F.

7. Place loaf pans on a baker's sheet, remove plastic wrap, and bake for 55–60 minutes, or until tops are deep-golden brown and internal temperature reaches 200–205°F (if tops of loaves are deep-golden brown, but internal temperature has not reached 200–205°F, cover loaves with foil to prevent over-browning).

Proofing Time: 5 hours   Bake Time: 55–60 minutes   Makes: Two 8" baras brith

It's the night BEFORE Bake Day (p. 58). As usual, you're going to pull 1/2 cup mother from your Refrigerator Mother, feed her 3/8 cup flour and 1/4 cup water, stir/cover, and put her back until next week.

To the 1/2 cup mother now in your *Glasslock* bowl that's about to become "activated batter," you'll add 3/8 cup flour and 1/4 cup water; stir/cover.

You'll also need to soak the dried fruit for this recipe. To do this, combine the ingredients listed in the chart below in a medium bowl, cover with plastic wrap, and refrigerate overnight.

Black Tea (brewed)	Honey	Raisins	Golden Raisins	Currants	Crystallized Ginger (diced)
2 cups	2 T	1/3 cup	1/3 cup	1/3 cup	1 T

It's Bake Day. Rise and shine! Feed your activated batter 3/8 cup flour and 1/4 cup water; stir/cover. Two to three hours later, it's ready to go to work for you.

Depending on the type of flour you're using, follow the amounts in the chart below.

	Activated Batter	Brown Sugar	Eggs	Orange Zest	Salt	Cinnamon	Nutmeg (ground)	Cloves (ground)	Flour (same type as mother)	B.F.M. Rice Starch*
White Rice	1 1/2 cups	1/4 cup	3	1 T	1 t	1 t	1/2 t	1/8 t	1 3/4 cups	1/2 cup
Brown Rice	1 1/2 cups	1/4 cup	3	1 T	1 t	1 t	1/2 t	1/8 t	2 3/4 cups	1/2 cup
Quinoa	1 1/2 cups	1/4 cup	3	1 T	1 t	1 t	1/2 t	1/8 t	5 cups	none

*Barron Flour Mill rice starch, p. 195

1. To the batter in your bowl, add dried fruit mixture (including the tea it was soaked in), brown sugar, eggs, orange zest, salt, cinnamon, nutmeg, and cloves; mix well.

2. Add flour (and rice starch, if using) to bowl with batter and mix until a stiff, tacky dough forms.

3. Generously butter two Norpro 8"L x 4.5"W x 3"H nonstick pans.

4. Evenly divide dough between prepared pans. Cover with plastic wrap and let rise in a warm place (70–73°F) for 3 hours, or until dough is level with the top of the pan.

5. Preheat oven to 350°F.

6. Place loaf pans on a baker's sheet, remove plastic wrap, and bake for 50–55 minutes, or until tops are deep-golden brown and internal temperature reaches 200–205°F (if tops of loaves are deep-golden brown, but internal temperature has not reached 200–205°F, cover loaves with foil to prevent over-browning).

White Rice

Proofing Time: 3 hours **Bake Time:** 50–55 minutes **Makes:** Two 8" baras brith

Yeast-leavened dough layered with butter, rolled, and then folded several times has been around forever. Whether or not the idea originated in France is easily debatable, because the same type of pastry has historical origins in many other countries. A *cornetto* with cappuccino is the most common breakfast in Italy. In Poland, they're filled with poppy seeds, almonds, raisins, and nuts. Argentines call it a *medialuna* (half moon). In other Spanish-speaking countries, it's called a *cureno* (horn). Wouldn't it be grand to go on a worldwide croissant-tasting tour?

(kruh SAHNT)
plural: croissants (same pronunciation; silent "s")

White

It's the night **BEFORE Bake Day** (p. 58). As usual, you're going to pull 1/2 cup mother from your Refrigerator Mother, feed her 3/8 cup flour and 1/4 cup water, stir/cover, and put her back until next week.

To the 1/2 cup mother now in your *Glasslock* bowl that's about to become "activated batter," you'll add 3/8 cup flour and 1/4 cup water; stir/cover.

It's Bake Day. Rise and shine! Feed your activated batter 3/8 cup flour and 1/4 cup water; stir/cover. Two to three hours later, it's ready to go to work for you.

Depending on the type of flour you're using, follow the amounts in the chart below.

	Activated Batter	Buttermilk	Honey	Butter (melted)	Eggs (separated)	Salt	Flour (same type as mother)
White	1 1/2 cups	1 cup	2 T	2 T	3	1 t	3 3/4 cups
Kamut	1 1/2 cups	1 cup	2 T	2 T	3	1 t	3 cups
Sprouted	1 1/2 cups	1 cup	2 T	2 T	3	1 t	3 3/4 cups
Einkorn	1 1/2 cups	1 cup	2 T	2 T	3	1 t	4 1/2 cups
Einka	1 1/2 cups	1 cup	2 T	2 T	3	1 t	3 3/4 cups

1. To the batter in your bowl, add buttermilk, honey, butter, 1 whole egg and 2 egg yolks (reserve whites for egg-white wash), and salt; mix well.

2. Reserve 1/2 cup flour for kneading. Add remaining flour to bowl with mother and mix until a stiff, tacky dough forms. Dust a clean work surface with reserved flour and scoop dough out of bowl. Knead dough until smooth and pliable (about 5 minutes).

3. Wash and dry bowl and coat with butter. Shape dough into a ball and add to bowl. Cover bowl with its lid and let condition in a warm place (70–73°F) for 2 hours.

4. Prepare Butter Filling Mix: In a small bowl, combine butter and flour; set aside.

Butter Filling Mix

Butter (softened)	Flour (same type as mother)
8 T	1/4 cup

5. Deflate dough and dust a clean work surface with flour. Roll dough out to 1/8" thickness. Evenly spread butter mixture over dough. Fold each edge toward the center so they are nearly touching, then fold the dough in half where the edges meet. Transfer to a baker's sheet, loosely cover with plastic wrap, and refrigerate for 20 minutes.

6. Roll the dough into a 1/8"-thick rectangle again, and fold each edge toward the center so they are nearly touching, then fold the dough in half where the edges meet. Place dough back on baking sheet, loosely cover with plastic wrap, and refrigerate for another 20 minutes (this process creates thin sheets of butter throughout the dough, which are responsible for all of the "layers" in the croissants). Repeat this process one more time.

7. Preheat oven to 350°F and line two baker's sheets with parchment paper.

8. Roll the dough into a 1/8"-thick rectangle that is 8" wide. Using a pastry wheel, cut into triangles that are 8" tall and 5" wide at the bottom. Starting from the bottom of a triangle, fold the two ends in to soften the points, then roll dough up and shape into a crescent. Transfer to prepared baking sheet and repeat with remaining triangles (re-rolling the dough will make tough croissants, so it's best to shape the odd-sized bits and bake them along with the croissants). Let croissants rest, uncovered, for 30 minutes.

9. In a small bowl, combine reserved egg whites and 2 t water. Mix until frothy, and strain mixture through a fine-mesh sieve to remove clumps (this makes a smooth, glossy finish on the croissants). Brush over croissants and bake for 15 minutes, rotating baking sheets halfway through. Remove from oven and brush with egg-white wash again. Bake an additional 5 minutes, or until golden brown and internal temperature reaches 200–205°F.

Kamut

PULL-APART PUMPKIN LOAF

Einka

White

It's the night BEFORE Bake Day (p. 58). As usual, you're going to pull 1/2 cup mother from your Refrigerator Mother, feed her 3/8 cup flour and 1/4 cup water, stir/cover, and put her back until next week.

To the 1/2 cup mother now in your *Glasslock* bowl that's about to become "activated batter," you'll add 3/8 cup flour and 1/4 cup water; stir/cover.

It's Bake Day. Rise and shine! Feed your activated batter 3/8 cup flour and 1/4 cup water; stir/cover. Two to three hours later, it's ready to go to work for you.

Depending on the type of flour you're using, follow the amounts in the chart below.

	Activated Batter	Pumpkin Purée	Milk	Maple Syrup	Eggs	Salt	Flour (same type as mother)
White	1 1/2 cups	1 cup	1/2 cup	1/3 cup	1	1 t	3 3/4 cups
Kamut	1 1/2 cups	1 cup	1/2 cup	1/3 cup	1	1 t	3 1/4 cups
Sprouted	1 1/2 cups	1 cup	1/2 cup	1/3 cup	1	1 t	3 1/2 cups
Einkorn	1 1/2 cups	1 cup	1/2 cup	1/3 cup	1	1 t	4 3/4 cups
Einka	1 1/2 cups	1 cup	1/2 cup	1/3 cup	1	1 t	4 3/4 cups

Sugar Coating

Sugar	Ground Cinnamon	Ground Nutmeg	Ground Cloves	Butter (melted)
1 1/2 cups	2 t	1/2 t	1/4 t	8 T

1. To the batter in your bowl, add pumpkin, milk, maple syrup, egg, and salt; mix well.

2. Reserve 1/2 cup flour for kneading. Add remaining flour to bowl with batter and mix until a stiff, tacky dough forms. Dust a clean work surface with reserved flour and scoop dough out of bowl. Knead dough until smooth and pliable (about 5 minutes).

3. Wash and dry bowl and coat with butter. Shape dough into a ball and add to bowl. Cover bowl with its lid and let condition in a warm place (70–73°F) for 2 hours.

4. Prepare Sugar Coating: In a medium bowl, combine sugar, cinnamon, nutmeg, and cloves. Mix well and set aside.

5. Preheat oven to 350°F, butter 4 mini loaf pans, and place pans on a baker's sheet.

6. Lightly dust a clean work surface with flour. Deflate dough and divide into 4 equal portions. Roll each portion out to a 6" x 15" rectangle. Cut rectangle into ten 3" squares. Brush squares with melted butter and dip in sugar mixture. Flip squares over and repeat.

7. Stack squares on top of each other and place into a prepared loaf pan. Repeat process with remaining portions of dough.

8. Loosely cover pans with plastic wrap and let rise in a warm place (70–73°F) for 30 minutes.

9. Remove plastic wrap and bake loaves on baking sheet for 30 minutes or until internal temperature reaches 200–205°F.

White

During our rigorous recipe testing process, we quickly discovered that when it comes to bread machines, there's a steep learning curve. Striking the balance between flour and liquid was our first challenge. Add too much flour, and you have a dry, dense loaf. Add too little flour, and loaves collapse in the middle during baking. Getting the proportions right proved especially problematic since the bread machine eliminates the need to knead bread dough by hand. Since we were well attuned to the tactile process of making bread, handing the job over to a machine took some getting used to (see our favorite in Section 5, Equipment, p. 208). After we tackled the flour/water balance issue, we discovered that certain flours made better breads with just water, while some were greatly improved with the addition of buttermilk, eggs or egg yolks, and butter. For this reason, we have created recipes that account for all these factors.

Why do these bread-machine recipes call for 4 cups of "activated batter"?

You'll note that the bread-machine recipes require 4 cups of activated batter rather than the 1 1/2 cups used throughout this section. This is largely because we prefer the taste and texture of bread-machine loaves with more batter. The other benefit to using more batter is that, throughout our tests, the bread simply rises more reliably and evenly in the bread machine with 4 cups of batter. To build your batter up to 4 cups before baking, follow the steps at right.

Bread Storage

I grew up in an era where snack foods were scarce, so our treats came from a shiny, metal breadbox sitting on my mother's kitchen counter. Without fail, she baked bread every week of her adult life. Plastic bags were also scarce, so her bread, once cooled, went directly into the breadbox, where the crust stayed crisp and the interior moist. The back of the lid was inlaid with wood and served as a cutting board; a bread knife lived just inside the hinged door. My uncle was a dairy farmer, so we had an abundance of milk and butter. Our go-to snack? Break up a slice of bread (preferably the crust or bread that had started to dry out) into bite-size chunks directly into a cereal bowl, fill the bowl with milk, drizzle honey or sugar on top, and grab a spoon.

It's the night BEFORE Bake Day (p. 58). As usual, you're going to pull 1/2 cup mother from your Refrigerator Mother, feed her 3/8 cup flour and 1/4 cup water, stir/cover, and put her back until next week. But to make a Bread-Machine Loaf, this is where your normal routine changes. To the 1/2 cup mother now in your *Glasslock* bowl that's about to become "activated batter," you'll add 2 1/4 cups flour and 1 1/2 cups water; stir/cover.

It's Bake Day. Rise and shine! Feed your activated batter 3/8 cup flour and 1/4 cup water; stir/cover. This will give you approximately 4 cups of batter. Two to three hours later, it's ready to go to work for you. This is the amount of batter you will need to make a single Bread-Machine Loaf.

Depending on the type of flour you're using, follow the amounts in the chart below.

	Activated Batter	Buttermilk	Eggs	Egg Yolks	Butter (melted)	Honey	Salt	Flour (same type as mother)	B.F.M. Rice Starch*
White	4 cups	1/4 cup	none	2	2 T	2 T	1 1/2 t	3 1/2 cups	none
Kamut	4 cups	1/4 cup	none	2	2 T	2 T	1 1/2 t	3 cups	none
Sprouted	4 cups	1/4 cup	none	2	2 T	2 T	1 1/2 t	3 3/4 cups	none
Einkorn	4 cups	1/4 cup	none	2	2 T	2 T	1 1/2 t	5 1/4 cups	none
Einka	4 cups	none	none	none	none	2 T	1 1/2 t	3 3/4 cups	none
White Rice	4 cups	none	2	none	none	2 T	1 1/2 t	1 1/4 cups	1/2 cup
Brown Rice	4 cups	none	2	none	none	2 T	1 1/2 t	2 1/2 cups	1/2 cup
Quinoa	4 cups	none	2	none	none	2 T	1 1/2 t	3 3/4 cups	none

*Barron Flour Mill rice starch, p. 195

1. Refer to the chart above for ingredients needed by type. In a large bowl, combine all ingredients called for, based on the type of flour you are using.

2. Mix until dough is thick and barely tacky; pour into bread-machine pan.

3. It is important to make a custom cycle on your bread machine that does not include a second knead and second rise. Times will vary on individual machines, but our *Zojirushi* machine is set for:

    Medium Crust
    Preheat: 5 minutes
    Knead: 10 minutes
    Rise #1: 2 hours, 20 minutes
    Bake: 1 hour, 10 minutes
This comes to a grand total of 3 hours, 45 minutes.

White Rice

4. Turn bread machine on, and once kneading cycle is complete, smooth out top of bread (it sometimes gets stuck in a balled-up shape). Then, let the bread-machine cycles complete.

5. Once bread is baked, remove from pan and transfer to a cooling rack.

Makes: One loaf

Kamut

Einkorn

Einka

Sprouted

Einka

It's the night BEFORE Bake Day (p. 58). As usual, you're going to pull 1/2 cup mother from your Refrigerator Mother, feed her 3/8 cup flour and 1/4 cup water, stir/cover, and put her back until next week.

To the 1/2 cup mother now in your *Glasslock* bowl that's about to become "activated batter," you'll add 3/8 cup flour and 1/4 cup water; stir/cover.

It's Bake Day. Rise and shine! Feed your activated batter 3/8 cup flour and 1/4 cup water; stir/cover. Two to three hours later, it's ready to go to work for you.

Depending on the type of flour you're using, follow the amounts in the chart below.

	Activated Batter	Water	Salt	Honey	Flour (same type as mother)
White	1 1/2 cups	1 cup	1 1/2 t	1 t	2 3/4–3 1/4 cups
Kamut	1 1/2 cups	1 cup	1 1/2 t	1 t	2 1/4–2 3/4 cups
Sprouted	1 1/2 cups	1 cup	1 1/2 t	1 t	2–2 1/2 cups
Einkorn	1 1/2 cups	1 cup	1 1/2 t	1 t	4 3/4–5 1/4 cups
Einka	1 1/2 cups	1 cup	1 1/2 t	1 t	4–4 1/2 cups

1. To the batter in your bowl, add water, salt, and honey; mix well. Starting with the smallest amount of flour in the chart, reserve 1 cup of it for kneading and add the rest of it to the bowl with the batter; mix until a stiff, tacky dough forms. Let rest 5 minutes.

2. Dust a clean work surface with reserved flour and scoop dough out of bowl. As you begin to work in the reserved flour, resist the urge to add more flour, as it will produce a dense loaf. Instead, very lightly coat your hands with cooking oil to prevent dough from sticking to your hands. If dough is still too sticky after reserved flour has been worked in, begin working in another 1/2 cup of flour. Continue to knead until dough is smooth, pliable, and slightly tacky (about 8 minutes).

3. Wash and dry bowl and coat with safflower oil. Add dough to bowl, cover bowl with its lid, and let rest in a warm place (70–73°F) for 30 minutes.

4. After 30 minutes, remove lid. Starting at the edge of the bowl, lift a portion of the dough toward the center of the bowl using a bowl scraper. Rotate the bowl, lift another portion, and fold it toward the center. Repeat until all edges have been folded toward the center (6–8 total folds). Cover bowl with lid and let rest again in a warm place (70–73°F) for 30 minutes. Repeat fold/rest two more times. Now, you're done with the folding process that conditions the dough so it rises well (step 6).

5. After the last 30 minutes, place a 5- to 6-qt lidded cast-iron Dutch oven in oven and preheat to 475°F.

6. Generously dust a clean work surface with flour and scoop dough from bowl using the bowl scraper. Shape dough into a ball, dusting with flour as needed. Cover with a flour-sack cotton towel and let rise in a warm place (70–73°F) for 30 minutes.

7. Remove Dutch oven from oven and lightly dust inside with flour. Place loaf into Dutch oven. Using a bread lame, make swift, superficial, diagonal slashes across loaf and cover with lid.

8. Bake for 20 minutes, remove lid, and bake an additional 10–15 minutes, or until crust is nicely browned and internal temperature reaches 190°F.

9. Remove loaf from Dutch oven and transfer to a cooling rack.

Proofing Time: 2 hours, 30 minutes **Bake Time:** 30–35 minutes **Makes:** One loaf

GLUTEN-FREE
ADVANCED DUTCH-OVEN BREAD

Tip: To brown the surface of white- or brown-rice Dutch-Oven bread (quinoa browns beautifully on its own), dissolve 1/2 t baking soda in 1/4 cup water. Transfer to a spray bottle and mist tops of loaves as recipe directs.

Quinoa

It's the night BEFORE Bake Day (p. 58). As usual, you're going to pull 1/2 cup mother from your Refrigerator Mother, feed her 3/8 cup flour and 1/4 cup water, stir/cover, and put her back until next week.

To the 1/2 cup mother now in your *Glasslock* bowl that's about to become "activated batter," you'll add 3/8 cup flour and 1/4 cup water; stir/cover.

It's Bake Day. Rise and shine! Feed your activated batter 3/8 cup flour and 1/4 cup water; stir/cover. Two to three hours later, it's ready to go to work for you.

Depending on the type of flour you're using, follow the amounts in the chart below.

	Activated Batter	Water	Salt	Honey	Flour (same type as mother)	B.F.M. Rice Starch*
White Rice	1 1/2 cups	1 1/2 cups	1 1/2 t	1 t	2 cups	1/2 cup
Brown Rice	1 1/2 cups	1 1/2 cups	1 1/2 t	1 t	3 1/2 cups	3/4 cup
Quinoa	1 1/2 cups	1 1/2 cups	1 1/2 t	1 t	4 3/4 cups	none

*Barron Flour Mill rice starch, p. 195

1. To the batter in your bowl, add water, salt, and honey; mix well.

2. Add about half the required flour (and the rice starch, if using). Mix until a tacky dough forms; let rest 5 minutes.

3. Mix in remaining flour (dough may seem dry, but will moisten and come together during conditioning).

4. Cover bowl with its lid and let rest in a warm place (70–73°F) for 30 minutes.

5. After 30 minutes, remove lid. Starting at the edge of the bowl, lift a portion of the dough toward the center of the bowl using a bowl scraper. Rotate the bowl, lift another portion, and fold it toward the center. Repeat until all edges have been folded toward the center (6–8 total folds). Cover bowl with lid and let rest again in a warm place (70–73°F) for 30 minutes. Repeat fold/rest two more times. Now, you're done with the folding process that conditions the dough so it will rise well (step 7).

6. After the last 30 minutes, place a 5- to 6-qt lidded cast-iron Dutch oven in center of oven and preheat to 475°F. Line an 8" banneton proofing basket with a flour-sack cotton towel (to prevent banneton-basket markings on finished loaf). Lightly dust towel with flour and set aside.

7. Lightly dust a clean work surface with flour and scoop dough from bowl using the bowl scraper. Shape dough into a large ball, pinching seams together at bottom of the ball. Place in prepared banneton basket, seam side facing up. Cover with a flour-sack cotton towel and let rise for 30 minutes.

8. Remove Dutch oven and lightly dust with flour. Using the cotton towel beneath the dough, carefully lift loaf from the banneton basket into the Dutch oven. Using a bread lame, make swift, superficial slashes across loaf and cover with lid.

9. Bake for 20 minutes; remove lid; spray with baking-soda mixture, if using (see tip at left); and bake an additional 10–15 minutes, or until crust is nicely browned and internal temperature reaches 190°F.

10. Remove loaf from Dutch oven and transfer to a cooling rack.

Tip: For easily transferring the large ball of dough to the Dutch oven, the dough is first placed in an 8" banneton proofing basket, allowed to rest while the oven is preheating, and then carefully tipped into the hot Dutch oven. This method eliminates the need to attempt to lift the delicate dough from the counter to the Dutch oven by hand.

Proofing Time: 2 hours, 30 minutes   Bake Time: 30–35 minutes   Makes: One loaf   **171**

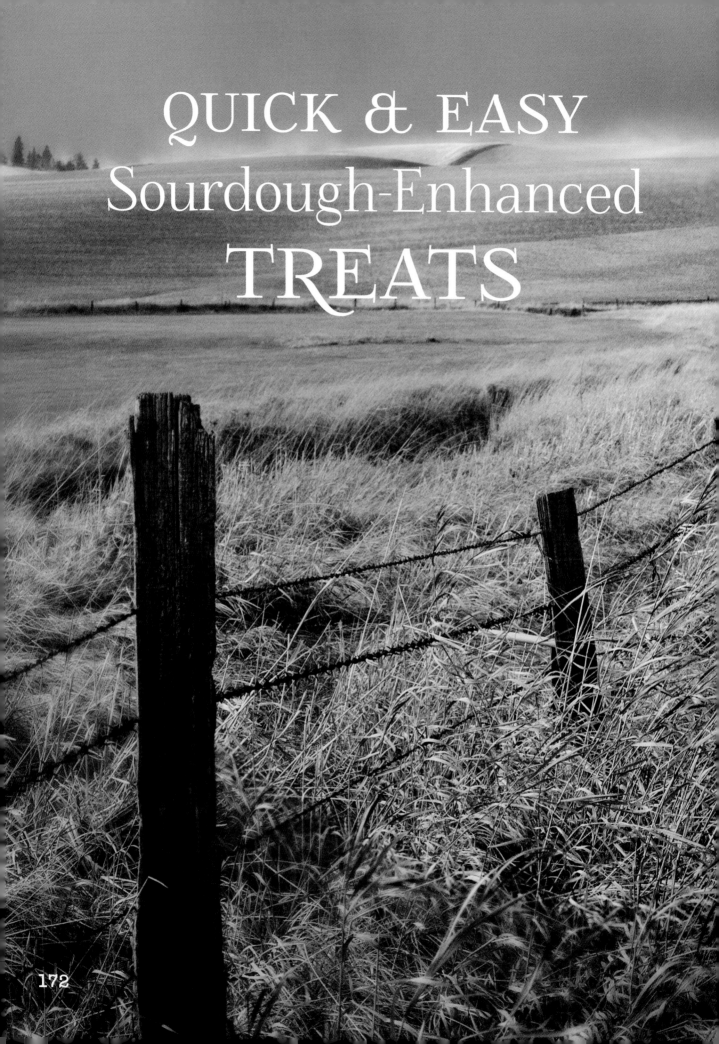

QUICK & EASY
Sourdough-Enhanced
TREATS

In This Section

*includes gluten-free versions

PANCAKES

White   Kamut   Einkorn   Brown Rice

Tip: We like storing our 1/2-cup portions of mother in 4-oz "Wean Green" baby-food glass storage containers. To thaw, we simply toss one into a large bowl of hot tap water (takes about 25 minutes). To thaw several, we put them in the refrigerator until thawed.

Einka

Sprouted

Quinoa

To make this sourdough-enhanced treat, it doesn't matter whether you're in the Counter or Refrigerator Mother phase, because no doubt, you've probably missed at least one Bake Day by now and followed our tip for portioning out your mother into handy 1/2-cup packages and tossed them into your freezer. Remember, it's okay to freeze portions of your mother because you won't be using it to give rise to bread, but to enhance the flavor and nutritive benefits of quick-and-easy treats like these pancakes that use baking powder for loft.

Depending on the type of flour you're using, follow the amounts in the chart below.

	Mother	Eggs	Buttermilk	Butter (melted)	Flour (same type as mother)	Sugar	Baking Powder	Salt
White	1 cup	1	1/4 cup	2 T	1/2 cup	1 T	1 t	1/4 t
Kamut	1 cup	1	1/4 cup	2 T	1/4 cup	1 T	1 t	1/4 t
Sprouted	1 cup	1	1/4 cup	2 T	1/4 cup	1 T	1 t	1/4 t
Einkorn	1 cup	1	1/4 cup	2 T	1/2 cup	1 T	1 t	1/4 t
Einka	1 cup	1	1/4 cup	2 T	1/2 cup	1 T	1 t	1/4 t
White Rice	1 cup	1	1/4 cup	2 T	1/4 cup	1 T	1 t	1/4 t
Brown Rice	1 cup	1	1/4 cup	2 T	1/2 cup	1 T	1 t	1/4 t
Quinoa	1 cup	1	1/4 cup	2 T	2/3 cup	1 T	1 t	1/4 t

1. In a small bowl, combine mother, egg, buttermilk, and butter; set aside.

2. In a medium bowl, combine flour, sugar, baking powder, and salt.

3. Add mother mixture to flour mixture and stir until smooth; set aside.

4. Preheat a large skillet or griddle over medium-low heat. Coat pan with butter and add 1/3 cup batter to pan. Cook for 2–4 minutes, or until center is bubbling and edges have lost their sheen. Flip over and cook an additional 2–4 minutes. Place cooked pancakes on a baker's half sheet and place in a 200° oven until ready to serve. Repeat with remaining batter.

Tip: This recipe can easily be doubled or even tripled. Freeze any extra pancakes in an airtight container between pieces of wax paper to reheat on days you need to hit the ground running.

Cook Time: 12–24 minutes **Makes:** Six 4" pancakes

White Rice

Tip: This recipe can easily be doubled or even tripled. Freeze any extra waffles in an airtight container between pieces of wax paper to reheat on days you need to hit the ground running.

Brown Rice

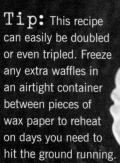

Old-fashioned waffle irons designed for use with wood cook stoves are perfect for our sourdough waffles. Set the lower compartment on top of campfire coals. The top part of the waffle iron is designed to swivel and turn above the hot coals for browning both sides.

To make this sourdough-enhanced treat, it doesn't matter whether you're in the Counter or Refrigerator Mother phase, because no doubt, you've probably missed at least one Bake Day by now and followed our tip for portioning out your mother into handy 1/2-cup packages and tossed them into your freezer. Remember, it's okay to freeze portions of your mother because you won't be using it to give rise to bread, but to enhance the flavor and nutritive benefits of quick-and-easy treats like these waffles that use baking powder for loft.

Depending on the type of flour you're using, follow the amounts in the chart below.

	Mother	Sugar	Eggs (separated)	Buttermilk	Butter (melted)	Flour (same type as mother)	Baking Powder	Baking Soda	Salt
White	2 cups	2 T	2	3/4 cup	2 T	1 3/4 cups	1 t	1 t	1/2 t
Kamut	2 cups	2 T	2	3/4 cup	2 T	1 cup	1 t	1 t	1/2 t
Sprouted	2 cups	2 T	2	3/4 cup	2 T	1 1/2 cups	1 t	1 t	1/2 t
Einkorn	2 cups	2 T	2	3/4 cup	2 T	2 cups	1 t	1 t	1/2 t
Einka	2 cups	2 T	2	3/4 cup	2 T	2 cups	1 t	1 t	1/2 t
White Rice	2 cups	2 T	2	1 cup	2 T	3/4 cup	1 t	1 t	1/2 t
Brown Rice	2 cups	2 T	2	3/4 cup	2 T	1 1/2 cups	1 t	1 t	1/2 t
Quinoa	2 cups	2 T	2	3/4 cup	2 T	1 1/2 cups	1 t	1 t	1/2 t

1. In a small bowl, combine mother, sugar, egg yolks (reserving egg whites for step 5), buttermilk, and butter.

2. In a medium bowl, combine flour, baking powder, baking soda, and salt.

3. Preheat waffle iron.

4. Add mother mixture to flour mixture and stir until smooth; set aside.

5. Whip egg whites into soft peaks and gently fold into batter.

6. Coat waffle iron with butter, add about 1/2 cup batter to waffle iron, and cook for 2–3 minutes on each side. Place cooked waffles on a baker's half sheet and place in a 200° oven until ready to serve. Repeat with remaining batter.

Cook Time: 24–48 minutes **Makes:** Six to eight waffles, depending on waffle-iron size and type of flour used

Quinoa

White

Craving something sweet and a little tangy? Well then, these sweet muffins with raspberries and lemon are just the thing. If your cravings take you down a different avenue, don't be afraid to swap the raspberries and lemon zest for fresh blueberries or even sautéed apples and cinnamon.

On p. 180, you'll find our all-time-farm-favorite: Savory Muffins. I daresay they are the best pesto muffins I've ever eaten. Regardless of your inclination toward sweet or savory, both these recipes are sure to have you coming back for more.

To make this sourdough-enhanced treat, it doesn't matter whether you're in the Counter or Refrigerator Mother phase, because no doubt, you've probably missed at least one Bake Day by now and followed our tip for portioning out your mother into handy 1/2-cup packages and tossed them into your freezer. Remember, it's okay to freeze portions of your mother because you won't be using it to give rise to bread, but to enhance the flavor and nutritive benefits of quick-and-easy treats like these muffins that use baking powder for loft.

Depending on the type of flour you're using, follow the amounts in the chart below.

	Mother	Sugar	Brown Sugar	Eggs	Butter (melted)	Vanilla Extract	Flour (same type as mother)	Baking Powder	Salt	B.F.M. Rice Starch*
White	1 cup	1/2 cup	1/4 cup	2	6 T	1 t	3/4 cup	2 t	1/2 t	none
Kamut	1 cup	1/2 cup	1/4 cup	2	6 T	1 t	3/4 cup	2 t	1/2 t	none
Sprouted	1 cup	1/2 cup	1/4 cup	2	6 T	1 t	3/4 cup	2 t	1/2 t	none
Einkorn	1 cup	1/2 cup	1/4 cup	2	6 T	1 t	1 cup	2 t	1/2 t	none
Einka	1 cup	1/2 cup	1/4 cup	2	6 T	1 t	3/4 cup	2 t	1/2 t	none
White Rice	1 cup	1/2 cup	1/4 cup	2	6 T	1 t	3/4 cup	2 t	1/2 t	2 T
Brown Rice	1 cup	1/2 cup	1/4 cup	2	6 T	1 t	3/4 cup	2 t	1/2 t	2 T
Quinoa	1 cup	1/2 cup	1/4 cup	2	6 T	1 t	1 1/4 cups	2 t	1/2 t	none

*Barron Flour Mill rice starch, p. 195

Raspberry Filling

Raspberries	Lemon Zest
1 cup	1 T

Icing (optional)

Powdered Sugar	Milk
1/2 cup	2 1/2 t

1. Preheat oven to 375°F. Line a 12-cavity muffin tin with paper liners and set aside.

2. In a medium bowl, combine mother, sugar, brown sugar, eggs, butter, and vanilla extract.

3. In a small bowl, combine flour, baking powder, and salt (and rice starch, if using). Add to mother mixture; mix well.

4. Using as few strokes as possible, fold in raspberries and lemon zest.

5. Spoon batter into paper liners until full and well-rounded.

6. Bake for 20–23 minutes, or until a toothpick inserted into the center of a muffin comes out clean.

7. Make Icing (optional): Combine powdered sugar and milk in a small bowl and mix until smooth. Drizzle over cooled muffins (we used a Wilton mini squeeze bottle) and let dry completely.

Cook Time: 20–23 minutes   **Makes:** Twelve muffins

White Rice

Brown Rice

White
Rice

To make this sourdough-enhanced treat, it doesn't matter whether you're in the Counter or Refrigerator Mother phase, because no doubt, you've probably missed at least one Bake Day by now and followed our tip for portioning out your mother into handy 1/2-cup packages and tossed them into your freezer. Remember, it's okay to freeze portions of your mother because you won't be using it to give rise to bread, but to enhance the flavor and nutritive benefits of quick-and-easy treats like these muffins that use baking powder for loft.

Cheese Filling

Extra-Sharp Cheddar Cheese (shredded)	Feta Cheese (crumbled)	Walnuts (coarsely chopped)	Basil Pesto
1 1/3 cup	2/3 cup	1/2 cup	2/3 cup

Depending on the type of flour you're using, follow the amounts in the chart below.

	Mother	Eggs	Butter (melted)	Lemon Juice	Flour (same type as mother)	Baking Powder	Salt	B.F.M. Rice Starch*
White	1 cup	2	4 T	1/2 t	1/2 cup	2 1/2 t	1/2 t	none
Kamut	1 cup	2	4 T	1/2 t	1/2 cup	2 1/2 t	1/2 t	none
Sprouted	1 cup	2	4 T	1/2 t	3/4 cup	2 1/2 t	1/2 t	none
Einkorn	1 cup	2	4 T	1/2 t	1 cup	2 1/2 t	1/2 t	none
Einka	1 cup	2	4 T	1/2 t	3/4 cup	2 1/2 t	1/2 t	none
White Rice	1 cup	2	4 T	1/2 t	1/2 cup	2 1/2 t	1/2 t	2 T
Brown Rice	1 cup	2	4 T	1/2 t	1/2 cup	2 1/2 t	1/2 t	2 T
Quinoa	1 cup	2	4 T	1/2 t	3/4 cup	2 1/2 t	1/2 t	none

*Barron Flour Mill rice starch, p. 195

1. Preheat oven to 375°F. Line a 12-cavity muffin tin with paper liners and set aside.

2. Prepare Cheese Filling: In a medium bowl, combine cheeses, walnuts, and pesto.

3. In another medium bowl, combine mother, eggs, butter, and lemon juice.

4. In a small bowl, combine flour, baking powder, salt (and rice starch, if using). Add to mother mixture; mix well.

5. Using as few strokes as possible, fold in cheese mixture.

6. Spoon batter into paper liners until full and well-rounded.

7. Bake for 22–25 minutes, or until a toothpick inserted into the center of a muffin comes out clean.

Cook Time: 22–25 minutes **Makes:** Twelve muffins

Quinoa ←

Brown Rice ←

Tip: Both our Savory Muffins and Sweet Muffins (prior page) can also be baked in three mini-loaf pans. Add approx. 10 minutes baking time.

Quinoa

Kamut

White
Rice

To make this sourdough-enhanced treat, it doesn't matter whether you're in the Counter or Refrigerator Mother phase, because no doubt, you've probably missed at least one Bake Day by now and followed our tip for portioning out your mother into handy 1/2-cup packages and tossed them into your freezer. Remember, it's okay to freeze portions of your mother because you won't be using it to give rise to bread, but to enhance the flavor and nutritive benefits of quick-and-easy treats like this kale dip with panbread bites that use baking powder for loft.

Kale Dip

Frozen Kale*	Butter	Yellow Onion (peeled and diced)	Garlic Cloves (peeled and minced)	Gruyère Cheese (shredded and divided)	Cream Cheese (softened)	Sour Cream	Cashews	Salt	Pepper
10 ozs	2 T	1 cup	1 T	1 1/2 cups	1 cup	2/3 cup	1/3 cup	3/4 t	1/2 t

*spinach also works great for this dip

Panbread Bites

Depending on the type of flour you're using, follow the amounts in the chart below.

	Mother	Water	Olive Oil	Honey	Flour (same type as mother)	Baking Powder	Baking Soda	Salt	B.F.M. Rice Starch*	Butter (melted)
White	1 cup	1/4 cup	1 1/2 T	1 1/2 T	1 1/4 cups	1 1/2 t	3/4 t	3/4 t	none	1 T
Kamut	1 cup	1/4 cup	1 1/2 T	1 1/2 T	1 1/4 cups	1 1/2 t	3/4 t	3/4 t	none	1 T
Sprouted	1 cup	1/4 cup	1 1/2 T	1 1/2 T	1 1/2 cups	1 1/2 t	3/4 t	3/4 t	none	1 T
Einkorn	1 cup	1/4 cup	1 1/2 T	1 1/2 T	2 cups	1 1/2 t	3/4 t	3/4 t	none	1 T
Einka	1 cup	1/4 cup	1 1/2 T	1 1/2 T	2 cups	1 1/2 t	3/4 t	3/4 t	none	1 T
White Rice	1 cup	1/2 cup	1 1/2 T	1 1/2 T	1 cup	1 1/2 t	3/4 t	3/4 t	2 T	1 T
Brown Rice	1 cup	1/4 cup	1 1/2 T	1 1/2 T	1 cup	1 1/2 t	3/4 t	3/4 t	2 T	1 T
Quinoa	1 cup	1/4 cup	1 1/2 T	1 1/2 T	1 1/2 cups	1 1/2 t	3/4 t	3/4 t	none	1 T

*Barron Flour Mill rice starch, p. 195

1. Make Kale Dip: Thaw kale and squeeze out as much water as you can (you should end up with about 1 cup of kale).

2. In a medium skillet over medium heat, cook butter, onion, and garlic until onion is soft (about 10 minutes); remove from heat.

3. Add kale, 1 cup Gruyère cheese, cream cheese, sour cream, cashews, salt, pepper, and onion mixture to a food processor; pulse until smooth.

4. Lightly butter a 15" x 12 1/4" cast-iron griddle. Preheat oven to 425°F.

5. Spread kale dip in a smooth layer onto prepared griddle; set aside.

6. Make Panbread: In a medium bowl, combine mother, water, olive oil, and honey.

7. In another medium bowl, combine flour, baking powder, baking soda, and salt (and rice starch, if using). Add to mother mixture; mix well.

8. Dust a clean work surface with flour and scoop dough out of bowl. Divide dough into 34 small pieces and shape each piece into a ball, dusting with flour as needed. Place shaped bread around the outer edge of griddle; brush with half the melted butter.

9. Sprinkle remaining 1/2 cup Gruyère over kale dip and bake for 15–18 minutes, or until kale dip is bubbling and panbread bites are golden brown. Brush bites with remaining melted butter.

Bake Time: 15–18 minutes Makes: 10–12 servings

from top:
White Rice
Brown Rice
Einkorn
Quinoa

To make this sourdough-enhanced treat, it doesn't matter whether you're in the Counter or Refrigerator Mother phase, because no doubt, you've probably missed at least one Bake Day by now and followed our tip for portioning out your mother into handy 1/2-cup packages and tossed them into your freezer. Remember, it's okay to freeze portions of your mother because you won't be using it to give rise to bread, but to enhance the flavor and nutritive benefits of quick-and-easy treats like these cake doughnuts that use baking powder for loft.

Depending on the type of flour you're using, follow the amounts in the chart below.

	Butter (softened)	Sugar	Mother	Milk	Eggs	Vanilla Extract	Flour (same type as mother)	Baking Powder	Salt	B.F.M. Rice Starch*
White	8 T	1/2 cup	1 cup	1/4 cup	2	1 t	2 1/2 cups	1 T	1/2 t	none
Kamut	8 T	1/2 cup	1 cup	1/4 cup	2	1 t	2 1/2 cups	1 T	1/2 t	none
Sprouted	8 T	1/2 cup	1 cup	1/4 cup	2	1 t	2 3/4 cups	1 T	1/2 t	none
Einkorn	8 T	1/2 cup	1 cup	1/4 cup	2	1 t	3 1/2 cups	1 T	1/2 t	none
Einka	8 T	1/2 cup	1 cup	1/4 cup	2	1 t	3 1/4 cups	1 T	1/2 t	none
White Rice	8 T	1/2 cup	1 cup	1/4 cup	3	1 t	2 cups	1 T	1/2 t	1/2 cup
Brown Rice	8 T	1/2 cup	1 cup	1/4 cup	3	1 t	3 cups	1 T	1/2 t	1/2 cup
Quinoa	8 T	1/2 cup	1 cup	1/4 cup	2	1 t	4 cups	1 T	1/2 t	none

*Barron Flour Mill rice starch, p. 195

Safflower Oil	Sugar	Cinnamon
4 cups	1 1/2 cups	1 T

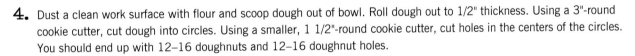

1. In a large bowl or stand mixer fitted with a flat beater, blend butter and sugar until light and fluffy.

2. Add mother, milk, eggs, and vanilla extract; mix well.

3. In medium bowl, combine flour, baking powder, and salt (and rice starch, if using). Add flour mixture to butter mixture and mix just until a firm, workable dough forms.

4. Dust a clean work surface with flour and scoop dough out of bowl. Roll dough out to 1/2" thickness. Using a 3"-round cookie cutter, cut dough into circles. Using a smaller, 1 1/2"-round cookie cutter, cut holes in the centers of the circles. You should end up with 12–16 doughnuts and 12–16 doughnut holes.

5. Add safflower oil to a 5- to 6-qt Dutch oven. Using a quick-read thermometer, heat oil over medium heat to 320–330°F.

6. While oil is heating, in a small bowl, mix together sugar and cinnamon for coating doughnuts; set aside.

7. Place a cooling rack inside a baker's sheet.

8. Once oil is hot, begin frying the doughnuts in small batches, leaving enough room in between each doughnut for flipping.

9. Cook doughnuts for 1 1/2–2 minutes. Using a stainless-steel skimmer, flip over and cook an additional 1 1/2–2 minutes, or until golden brown.

10. Remove doughnuts from Dutch oven and place on prepared cooling rack. Allow doughnuts to sit for about 30 seconds, then, one at a time, place into the bowl with the cinnamon/sugar coating. Flip several times, spooning sugar over doughnuts to coat. Place coated doughnuts back on cooling rack.

11. Repeat this process until all doughnuts and doughnut holes have been fried and coated.

Cook Time: 15–24 minutes **Makes:** 12–16 doughnuts and doughnut holes, depending on type of flour used **185**

One of the things I like about stirring a sourdough mother is the time-machine effect her essence, her smell evokes. Whenever I try to remember details from the years I worked in remote locations for the Forest Service, it's, well, effort, and they're just details, a lot like perfunctory list-making or squinting your eyes to help with focus. But a smell trigger is like an astral projection of sorts, and many times more powerful. You're not trying to remember, you're there again.

My "there" might be the 14' x 16' canvas wall tent I lived in year-round in the remote Selway-Bitterroot Wilderness area, 25 miles from the end of a dirt road, without modern conveniences like electricity or flush toilets, accessible only by horse, foot, or small airplane. Sometimes, it's the one-room cabin at the base of a 100-foot fire-watch tower in northern Idaho, or the green, canvas base-camp tent I called home while working as one of the first female Wilderness Rangers in the U.S.

In those locations, my life was, no doubt, less complex than it is now. And I was often alone, but in a good way—not lonely, just alone. Come to think of it, maybe that's the reason my living, breathing, sourdough mother was such an important part of my life back then. She nurtured me, and in return, I cared for her. But there was more to it than that. Within the circle of people that I did interact with—family members who visited, occasional firefighters, trail-crew members I drank coffee with around a campfire, stray backpackers, horseback riders, airplane pilots, and backcountry outfitters—I became known for my sourdough chocolate cake. Serving a slice of cake and a cup of camp coffee to visitors turned into a preoccupation, a calling.

Groceries were either carried in on my back, delivered by pack train, or flown in on a Cessna airplane. While living in the Selway, it was my job to make sure the pack horses and mules were called off the pasture before the supply plane landed, all of them corralled and accounted for. And because I didn't have electricity, I stored the cream cheese, eggs, and butter in an evaporative cooler—really, just a fancy name for a screened box with gunnysack sides that wicked water down from a dishpan on top that I kept full of water. A nearby root cellar served as a backup.

My sourdough mother lived on a bare wooden countertop next to a summer sink with gravity-fed cold running water from a nearby creek. Handy for making pancakes and skillet bread, she was most happy in the winter because spending a winter in a wall tent meant I kept a fire stoked night and day. With sometimes as much as five feet of insulating snow up the sides of my tent, we were cozy and warm.

I grew up with the words "wall tent," but on occasion, the phrase draws a blank look. A wall tent is more than just a tent—it's a temporary home: four walls and sometimes, running water. I came across the photo below in my mother-in-law's scrapbook; it depicts what it was like growing up in rural Idaho in the '30s, only a few miles from where I now live. Hasn't everyone, at some time or another, daydreamed of their own little escape cabin, somewhere away from it all? It doesn't take much to get a tent flap flying in the wind, a fire banked in a wood cookstove, and a bubbly, very-much-alive, wild mother started for unforgettable slices of sourdough chocolate cake (p. 188).

To make this sourdough-enhanced treat, it doesn't matter whether you're in the Counter or Refrigerator Mother phase, because no doubt, you've probably missed at least one Bake Day by now and followed our tip for portioning out your mother into handy 1/2-cup packages and tossed them into your freezer. Remember, it's okay to freeze portions of your mother because you won't be using it to give rise to bread, but to enhance the flavor and nutritive benefits of quick-and-easy treats like this chocolate cake that use baking powder for loft.

	Butter (softened)	Sugar	Cocoa Powder	Eggs	Vanilla Extract	Mother	Flour (same type as mother)	Baking Powder	Salt
White	1 cup	2 3/4 cups	1 cup	5	2 t	5 cups	1 cup	1 T	1 t

Frosting

Cream Cheese	Honey	Cocoa Powder
6 cups (about 48 oz)	1/2 cup	3/8 cup

1. Preheat oven to 350°F. Line the bottoms of four 8" cake pans with parchment paper. Generously butter inside edges of pans and dust with flour; set aside.

2. In a large bowl or stand mixer fitted with a flat beater, cream butter, sugar, and cocoa powder together.

3. Add eggs, one at a time, mixing well after each addition and scraping bowl as needed. Add vanilla extract and mix well.

4. Add sourdough mother to butter mixture. Mix until a smooth, creamy batter forms, scraping bowl as needed.

5. In a small bowl, combine flour, baking powder, and salt. Add to butter mixture and mix well.

6. Evenly divide batter between prepared cake pans and bake all four at once for 25–30 minutes, or until a toothpick inserted into the center of cakes comes out clean. Cool cakes completely on cooling racks (about 1 1/2 hours).

7. If you're in a hurry to get your cake frosted, line two baking sheets with parchment or wax paper and transfer cakes to baking sheets. Freeze for 1 hour to firm the cakes for easy frosting.

8. Make Frosting: In a large bowl or stand mixer fitted with a flat beater, mix cream cheese and honey together, scraping bowl as needed. Add cocoa powder and blend until smooth.

9. Assemble: Remove parchment paper from bottoms of cake layers. Place one layer on serving platter and add 1 1/4 cups frosting. Spread frosting out into a smooth, level layer and add another cake layer. Repeat process with remaining cake layers. Once all layers are stacked, use remaining frosting to frost top and sides of cake.

Prep Time: 45 minutes, plus 2 1/2 hours cooling time

Bake Time: 25–30 minutes

Makes: One 8" layer cake

LET'S TALK FLOUR

and Specialty Ingredients

In This Section

LET'S TALK FLOUR

In this photo, you can see my farm in the foreground and then endless acres of wheat that continue as far as the eye can see. I live in wheat country, in the well-known "wheat belt" that extends along a north-south axis for more than 1,500 miles from where I am, close to the Canadian border, all the way to central Texas. Historically, farmers here in northern Idaho grew a variety of crops, but when the market for soft white wheat shipped to the Orient showed promise, acres upon acres of farmland were converted to wheat production. As

a young man, my father-in-law joined in, harvesting wheat first with a team of horses and then eventually, with a gas-powered combine. As I type this, I can look out my window and see his abandoned horse-drawn equipment that my children used as a jungle gym when they were young.

The heirloom wheat I grew (center) compared to modern varieties.

But too many people hungry for massive amounts of a single commodity has its downside when it comes to production because when my father-in-law was still alive, he talked about the black clouds of "smut" lifting from the fields, the chaff and grain transformed by disease into a toxic black powder that dusted everything in sight. Along the way, local agricultural land-grant colleges jumped in to help. Modern wheat is the result of researchers who played around with wheat genetics until they'd not only controlled things like black mold, leaf rust, and powdery mildew, but they'd also engineered larger wheat kernels and higher crop yields.

Wheat mold, rust, and mildew were controlled but not eradicated, because when I decided to grow a small crop of heirloom varieties of wheat one summer, I also grew a decent crop of mold, rust, and mildew on my plants, as you can see below, from the photos I took.

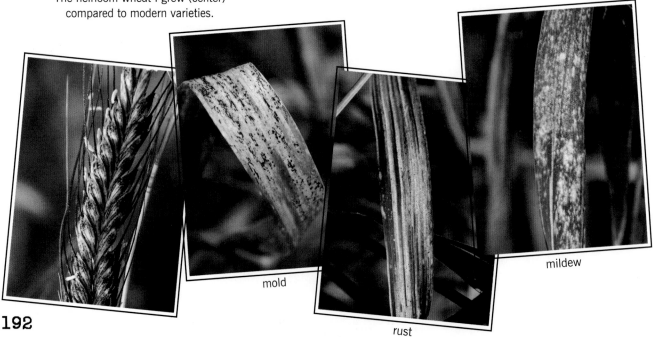

mold

rust

mildew

My understanding of why heirloom varieties were abandoned experienced a growth spurt. Every time I receive a shipment of Einka® organic heirloom whole-wheat flour from BluebirdGrainFarms.com in nearby Winthrop, Washington, I'm grateful and in awe of the work it must take to supply me and, hopefully, you with their incredibly fresh, organic flour. They seem to have perfected rotational cover crops and the timing of tillage and planting. Also, they irrigate their wheat crop, giving them more control over its growth while lessening stress-induced diseases. Plus, they condition their grain in custom-built, wooden granaries so that moisture in the grain is absorbed by the wood, preventing mold and fungal diseases. And their grains are cleaned and milled to order in small batches each week. Overall, their flour is a delight to work with and, without fail, produces high-quality breads for us. When compared to white flour, the loaves are slightly denser, but that's to be expected because Einka is a whole-wheat flour. Breads made with Einka flour have a tender crumb and are packed with flavor, as if you'd grabbed a handful of grain from a wheat stalk and tossed it into your mouth.

When we first started working with einkorn organic heirloom wheat (also heirloom, but with 80 percent of the bran and germ removed), we were wildly impressed with the results. Our breads rose high and had a delicious, faintly nutty flavor and a gorgeous, pale-golden color. But along the way, we started to note that the quality of the rise began to deteriorate, as did our confidence in the reliability of the flour. After plenty of brainstorming and testing, we finally landed on a simple question: Was our most recent batch of flour not up to par? After ordering and receiving a new batch of einkorn flour, we eagerly set to work mixing up a batch of dough. Right away, it was obvious that this batch of flour was better. The dough was stretchy and elastic again, whereas batches of dough from our previous lot of einkorn flour were clay-like and didn't hold their shape well. Both flours were ordered directly from JovialFoods.com, and both had expiration dates months away, so rancidity in the first batch was not the issue. (REMEMBER, you can always test for rancidity by putting a bit of flour on your tongue; if it's at all bitter, toss it.) The simplest explanation for the lot of einkorn that wasn't optimal for baking bread? As a crop, wheat is subject to the vagaries of weather. Jovial Foods' heirloom einkorn grain is grown in Italy using a method called "dryland farming" (without irrigation) so they might have had too little rain. Just as some years are great for my crop of garlic, others aren't. Wheat is subject to the same environmental incidentals. When you live in wheat country like I do, you're surrounded by ongoing conversations regarding weather and its effect on the quality of wheat from year to year.

Once we had the flour-quality issue sorted out, our breads were greatly improved, but still not producing the beautiful breads we created from our first lot of einkorn. We continued to troubleshoot and experiment.

All of that led to three helpful einkorn pointers.

1. The first is that, although einkorn is processed in much the same way as white flour, the dough handles differently. Einkorn takes longer to absorb liquids. For this reason, it's tempting to continue to add flour to the sticky dough, but when we did, we ended up with dense, cakey, even flour-flaked loaves. So, before you grab more flour to fix the stickiness of your einkorn dough, give the dough a little time to rest and absorb the liquid.

2. The second is that the protein composition of einkorn is different from that of modern wheat. In the simplest of terms, this means the gluten needs a little help developing. This can be achieved by folding the dough during the first conditioning stage, just like the process detailed for making Bâtards (p. 62). Later, as we moved away from French and Italian breads and into enriched breads, the folding technique was not used. However, if you are having trouble with formless, sticky, einkorn loaves, revert to the folding process during the conditioning stage and the quality of your loaves will improve.

3. The third pointer is to blend it. Our biggest disappointment came when we made einkorn bagels. But that happened during use of the lot that we decided wasn't up to par. However, during the time we were troubleshooting and trying different things, we started cutting the flour half-and-half with Einka (so we could stick with heirloom grains), and that solved the problem. So, if you end up with a batch of einkorn that performs differently from your previous batch, follow the tips above or blend it with some Einka. (continued)

(continued from p. 193)

Of all the flours we use, `Kamut® (Khorasan) organic heirloom whole-wheat flour` is the most delightful to work with. The flour has a sandy texture that readily mixes into doughs and isn't ever sticky—its lack of stickiness is most notable when stirring a Kamut mother. Belying the sandy texture of the flour, it creates a dough that is smooth and elastic and handles exceedingly well. Breads made with Kamut have a buttery, yellow cast and are moist and supple, never gritty. Kamut flour is an absolute pleasure to handle. I've been making breads with it for some 20 years. Find it at `MontanaFlour.com.` (Note: They also sell a version of Kamut flour that has 20 percent of the bran removed; we use the 100 percent whole-wheat version.) To read a heartwarming story about the farmer behind Kamut, go to Kamut.com.

After working with `organic white-wheat flour (unbleached)` alongside so many other different flours, it's easy to understand why it became the flour of choice for mass bread production. With minimal encouragement, it develops a strong gluten structure and is easy to work with. Its rise is reliable and substantial. If I had to choose between white flour and whole-wheat flour that has any percentage of rancidity, either developing or full-blown, I'd choose white flour every time. Rancid oils wreak havoc in our bodies. They've been linked to advanced aging and neurological disorders. They're carcinogenic, pro-inflammatory, and just plain toxic.

When flour was no longer purchased from your local mill, like in Joseph's childhood, white flour became necessary because flour traveled long distances and then sat on store shelves. Whole-wheat flour should be thought of as a fresh vegetable that needs to be eaten … well, fresh. White flour lessens that need, which is probably the reason Jovial Foods removes 80 percent of the bran and germ. They chose shelf life over whole wheat. I think it was probably a good decision, given the size and reach of their business.

Ever since I learned milling alongside Joseph, I've continued to provide customers with his `Barron Flour Mill Organic White Flour (Specialty Unbleached)`. Sourced in Montana, every batch is tested for reliability, and the grains that are used must meet a high standard of quality. Tried and true, it'll never disappoint. When it comes to bread making, I want to make sure everyone has access to at least one basic flour that I can oversee to make sure it will work for wild-bread making. First-time bread makers need to meet up with success. It's like offering a first-time gardener a packet of notoriously-easy-to-grow zucchini seeds. `Barron Flour Mill Organic White Flour (Specialty Unbleached)` is available at `WildBread.net.`

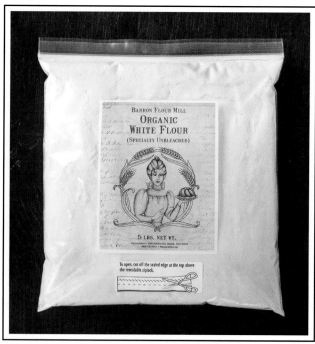

Comparable to white wheat in manageability, `organic sprouted hard red wheat flour,` available at `HealthyFlour.com,` makes loaves with surprisingly good loft but with an earthy flavor. I like the idea behind sprouted flours, and have successfully created organic sprouted brown-rice flour; organic sprouted quinoa flour (using a rainbow of different types, everything from red quinoa to golden); and organic sprouted whole-wheat flour using either Kamut, Einka, or einkorn kernels. Keep in mind, you can't sprout a grain that's been processed, like white rice. As long as the grain has been left whole without being hulled, it can be sprouted. See p. 198 for my how-to details on sprouting and milling grains in your own home. It's easy!

Perhaps the biggest adjustment to working with gluten-free flours is the absence of gluten. Kneading the dough doesn't help develop a gluten structure, because it isn't there to begin with. This can be thought of as a benefit, but it also means a little finesse is necessary when working with gluten-free doughs.

When working with **organic white-rice flour from BobsRedMill.com,** the lack of gluten makes the dough more delicate and prone to crumble. Doughs with higher liquid-to-flour ratios, like our batter breads in the beginner section, are best, because the starches in the dough swell during baking and absorb a lot of the moisture. Breads made with white rice have a crispy crust and soft, chewy interior, the flavor reminiscent of sticky rice but with a sourdough kick. Once you've moved into our advanced section, you'll find that some of our recipes don't offer our usual gluten-free alternative. Believe me, we tried. One of the things I didn't want to resort to when offering gluten-free recipes is to throw in the kitchen sink like you see in so many gluten-free breads and recipes—industrial-type binders like xanthum gum, guar gum, and gelatin, as well as a host of non-organic starches like corn, tapioca, and potato, and things like grain-sweet white sorghum flour, barley malt, and more. I wondered out loud to my DIL Ashley, "Isn't there some *one* thing we can add that will improve its pliability?" For wild-bread making, the magic ingredient was hiding in one of my backpacking foods all along. It worked like a charm. Initially, we thought that rather than have you come to us for it, we'd see if commonly available rice starch would work, but it didn't. Our organic rice starch that we put in our *MaryJane's Outpost* Instant Organic Bavarian Chocolate Mousse goes through a process in which it's heated first, then dried, creating an instant binder or gelling agent. You'll see **B.F.M. (Barron Flour Mill) Rice Starch** listed in most of the gluten-free rice bread recipes throughout our advanced section, **available at WildBread.net.**

Similar to working with white-rice flour, **organic brown-rice flour** is another delicate dough that requires a gentle hand. Like white-rice, brown-rice doughs with a higher moisture content, like our batter bread recipes in the beginner section, make the best breads. Brown-rice breads have a crisp crust and tender interior. Of all the bread recipes that we've perfected in the making of this book, the rice breads are my husband's favorite, and he's not even a gluten-free eater. They're that good. Organic brown-rice flour is available at **EdenFoods.com, TrueFoodsMarket.com,** and **BobsRedMill.com.**   (continued)

Flour Storage

One day when I was working alongside Joseph and milling dehydrated garbanzo-bean flakes for use in an instant, just-add-water hummus mix I was selling in my backpacking line at the time (I've since converted my hummus to black-bean hummus because I kept having shelf-life problems, even though I'd rented a commercial freezer in town to store them after I'd milled them; garbanzo beans are very high in oil), he tapped me on the shoulder, "If you put that in plastic bags, it'll sweat and then sour." I replied, "But, these are the sacks it came in." Joseph said, "Hell, I don't know that for sure."

That's how I've felt sometimes when people ask me how to best store their flour. Plastic? Paper? Freezer? I don't like the idea of a freezer because people put it in the freezer, thinking they've stopped it from going bad, but I believe it loses its freshness faster in a freezer than in a cool environment. Some say you can leave it in a freezer for no more than two or three months, but for making wild bread, storing flour in a freezer doesn't work for the same reason you can't put your mother in a freezer; it seems to harm the naturally occurring critters found on grain that are conducive to wild-bread making. So, for storage, I prefer a well-sealed plastic or glass container (we recommend a **Progressive flour keeper with built-in leveler**) and basic refrigeration rather than a freezer. **We store our flours in an old refrigerator dedicated to flour only and we mill or buy only what we need rather than stock up.** But mainly, I want to emphasize: Know where your flour comes from and make sure it's been recently milled. If that isn't possible, mill it yourself. We need to start thinking of flour as a fresh food, especially whole-grain flours that haven't had any of their oils removed.

(continued from p. 195)

When we first started a quinoa-flour Counter Mother with pre-milled, **`organic sprouted quinoa flour`** purchased online, we were impressed with how quickly the mother began to bubble, and how active it stayed. Once our Counter Mother was active enough to use in a loaf of Beginner Batter Bread, we eagerly watched and waited as the bread rose so we could have our first taste.

Much to our amazement, the bread rose like a gluten-based-flour bread, even though it lacks gluten. Once the bread was baked and cooled, we had our first taste. After a few chews, the disappointment set in—it was bitter. So, we began to troubleshoot.

What made the bread bitter? Even though we were offered reassurances from its makers, "Quinoa is naturally bitter, so you need to blend it with other flours," we knew that modern-day quinoa manufacturers pre-rinse it to remove the outer coating that used to give quinoa a bitter aftertaste. But that bitter taste associated with quinoa is a thing of the past. I love to cook with quinoa, so I buy a fair amount at our local co-op from their bulk bin, and it's never bitter. Rancid flour being the primary suspect, we began to mill quinoa grains into flour ourselves. We also started sprouting quinoa, drying it, and milling it into flour. From our freshly milled grains, we started four Counter Mothers using golden quinoa (golden is sometimes referred to as white), sprouted golden quinoa, rainbow quinoa (simply a combination of different kinds of quinoa), and sprouted rainbow quinoa flours. Our Counter Mothers became active quickly, and when Bake Day came around, we waited with nervous anticipation for our first taste. Much to our delight, the breads had a distinct quinoa flavor, but no bitterness! The golden quinoa loaves had a buttery-yellow hue, while the rainbow quinoa loaves had a wonderful dark, rye appearance. All of them had a light, airy crumb. To our great satisfaction, breads made with quinoa have continued to exceed our expectations. For this reason, creating wild bread using only quinoa flour remains an amazing discovery for us. We feel like true-blue pioneers.

QUINOA

WHITE RICE

WHOLE WHEAT

BROWN RICE

WHITE FLOUR

SPROUTED WHEAT

HEIRLOOM WHEAT

And we'd like you to feel the same way. It was necessary for us to limit the number of different flours we used so we could wrap our arms around the concept of wild-bread making without wading through too many variables (this book was ten years in the making as it is).

Jovial Foods now offers sprouted einkorn flour that we haven't yet tried. And Bluebird Grain Farms is offering flours with names like emmer and Pasayten that show promise. Or maybe teff, sorghum, spelt, triticale, and wild rice would work. I suspect there are even more wonderful grains, perhaps in a seed bank somewhere, or in a rusty can in a garden shed, awaiting discovery. **`Stay away from flours with additives and things like dough conditioners.`** We tried a well-known brand of organic whole-wheat flour that simply would not work. As it turns out, they add barley malt to the flour without listing it on the label.

The type of bread that is best for you may have to do with your physiological makeup. Perhaps the question isn't what bread is best but instead, what bread is best for you. Hop onto our chatroom and tell us about your wild-bread making. Ashley and I will continue to ponder and play and along the way, share our next phase of wild-bread making online at WildBread.net. **`Keep your eyes open, your heart engaged, and your hands in some flour.`**

One of the things I want to attempt is to try my hand at not only growing a small, artisan stand of wheat, but also to create a good system for threshing it. I'd like to use the turn-of-the-century, handmade, hand-crank thresher I have stored in my barn and get it working again.

In 2008, when I first launched my idea for wild-yeast bread making, one of the threads that popped up on my chatroom was a book suggestion for me to write: *Grow Your Own Wheat for Breadmaking*. One of our members, a woman named Lani from New Mexico, wrote this:

"My great-grandmother in Virginia grew her own wheat. When I knew her, she was in her later years, so she no longer cut and shocked the wheat herself, but she still whipped the wheat heads (literally, with a switch) to shell the grain. Next, she washed the chaff away in the creek in a basket, then dried it, and then ground it in an old coffee grinder she used just for wheat. In the mountains here in New Mexico, the wheat is laid out on the ground, and then a herd of goats or sheep are run around on top of it to shell it out. The wheat and chaff is swept up, put in a pan or basket shaped like a wok and tossed in the air for the breeze to blow away the chaff. Then, it's picked for stones, etc. and then washed, dried, and taken to the mill, and part of it traded to pay for the milling."

And Jan from San Jose, California, wrote: "We grew our own wheat for a 4-H project. We sowed it and then raked the plot lightly, so the soil covered the seed. Then we watered it as if we were planting a lawn. When the wheat was brown and dry and the seed heads nice and plump, we cut the heads off. We used hedge clippers over a container to collect them. Then, we put the wheat heads between two sheets of cloth and used a rolling pin on the wheat heads. This separated the wheat berries from the husk. After that, we poured the wheat berries and chaff in a container in front of a blowing fan. The chaff blew away. Next, we ground the wheat and baked bread."

Growing your own wheat, threshing it, and then turning it into bread is the ultimate full circle endeavor. Anyone else up to the challenge? If so, please share every detail at WildBread.net.

197

MAKE YOUR OWN SPROUTED FLOUR

Because I've had mixed results trying to *buy* organic sprouted flour (the quinoa and brown-rice sprouted flours I've purchased were bitter, hence rancid), I wanted to come up with a system for sprouting grains that was **simple, inexpensive, and efficient.**

To sprout wheat, rice, or quinoa, I use the following:

- [ ] 10-quart stockpot with handles and a lid
- [ ] 28" x 28" piece of cheesecloth
- [ ] dough scraper (for stirring)
- [ ] food dryer (for grains, use a temperature anywhere from 125°F–140°F)

I put 5–7 lbs of grains in a stockpot and cover with water roughly **twice the volume** of the grain, put the lid on, and leave it to soak overnight.

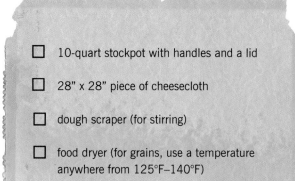

The next morning, **I rinse** the grains by putting the pot in my kitchen sink and running a thin stream of water into the pot while I gently stir the grains using a spatula. With heavier grains like rice that aren't likely to float to the top with the rising level of water, you don't have to be as careful about losing any down the drain. You're trying to "freshen" the moisture so the grains don't sour, because from this point on, the grains will no longer be soaking in standing water, but rather in a moist environment conducive to sprouting.

To drain the pot, put cheesecloth over the top. I wrap the cheesecloth around the handles. Then, I turn the pot into the sink and drain it until all the rinse water is out, shaking the grains stuck to the cheesecloth back into the pot. As is usually the case, nary a grain is lost.

I rinse the grains at least three times per day, four if it's summer and the weather is warmer.

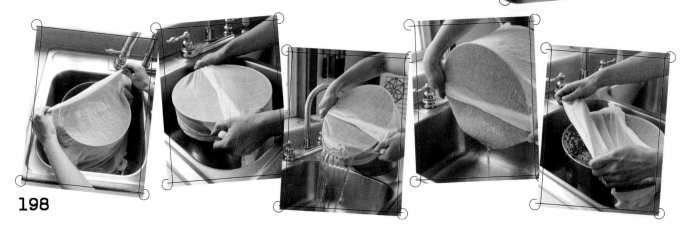

Once the grains show me the **mere hint of a sprout,** they're ready to become "sprouted flour." (Depending on the grain, this can take anywhere from 1–3 days.) No need to wait until you see sprouts on every single grain. As long as you can see tiny sprouts on most of the grains, the sprouting process that releases the grains' powerhouse of nutrients has taken place on all the grains.

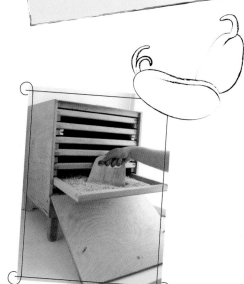
Sprouted Rice

I give them one last good rinse, and **into the dryer they go.** I leave openings amongst the grains so the hot air from the heating element at the bottom can get to the upper shelves. Because I prefer a dryer without a fan, I stir them several times throughout the day.

I also rotate the shelves, bottom to top, whenever I stir them. I set my style of dryer between medium and high. Once I've rotated all the shelves at least twice, I turn it to low. I continue to rotate, but not as frequently, until I'm convinced every grain is dry.

Next, I mill my sprouted grains.

See Section 5, Equipment, for information on my food dryer (p. 209), flour mill (p. 208), and wooden dough scraper (p. 206).

As I mill them, I put the flour into a large bowl and stir it occasionally until it has cooled off completely. Once cooled, I put the flour into an airtight container that goes into my fridge. The name of the game here is **FRESH, not rancid.** If you think a flour might have had the opportunity to go rancid, do the taste test. **Put a little on your tongue, and if it tastes bitter, toss it.**

WonderMill grain mill, p. 208

Quinoa, a gluten-free seed (pseudo grain) is very high in protein, has a natural coating (saponin) that tastes bitter (to discourage birds from dining on it). However, gone are the days in which we're told to rinse it several times before use. Most modern-day manufacturers have developed systems to rinse the bitter off so we don't have to. Clear-running water is an indication that they've done a good job rinsing (and then drying) it. Quinoa flour should never taste bitter. Not only was your quinoa probably rinsed before you purchased it, you'll rinse it several more times should you decide you want to make sprouted quinoa flour/bread. If you buy quinoa flour (both sprouted and un-sprouted) that tastes bitter when made into bread, don't let anyone tell you it's because quinoa is naturally bitter. The flour has gone rancid if your bread tastes bitter. The "prewashed" golden quinoa we purchased from the bulk bin at our local food co-op and milled ourselves without any rinsing at all was not bitter when made into bread. Likewise, the very same quinoa, when sprouted and then milled, did not have a bitter taste.

EQUIPMENT

Find it, buy it! Not all
equipment, cookware, and tools
are created equal.
Lean in for the lowdown.

Also, gift ideas.

For the same reason we share our favorite books, movies, and
occasionally, fishing holes, I want you to be able to playfully gift
the wonders and health benefits of wild bread.

In This Section

Equipment Checklist Details

Items discussed here are commonly available online (simply use the specific name we've provided for an online search) or check with your local kitchen store.

3.75-qt *Glasslock* 10 1/2"W x 5 1/2"H Mixing Bowl

We recommend this specific bowl because there are strict parameters for things like top and bottom width, height, and volume—and yes, even the curve of the bowl— that matter for maintaining a Counter Mother. Plus, it comes with a plastic lid that you'll use repeatedly in our Advanced Section.

10 1/2" *Marinex* Baking Dish

Once we found the perfect glass bowl for maintaining a Counter Mother, we started searching for its mate. The *Glasslock* needed a bottom dish that allowed for just the right amount of room to tuck in a flour-sack cotton towel without being so wide that it lets too much of the water evaporate. As far as arranged marriages go, this companion is perfect for your mother.

2-qt *Pyrex* Bakeware Dishes with Lids

When creating recipes for the Beginner Section, we tried everything from loaf pans to cast-iron skillets. In the end, we settled on glass because breads baked in glass form such a fabulous crust, plus it's fun to see your bread forming bubbles as it rises in addition to watching it form a crisp crust as it bakes. Then, we decided an oven-proof dish with a glass lid would be perfect for maintaining moisture during proofing. But, there was the volume problem. What would work perfectly for two loaves once Bake Day rolled around? When we finally tried the 2-qt *Pyrex* Bakeware Dish, Ashley and I gave each other high fives, because two of them also fit into the *Brød and Taylor* proofer (with the help of the shelf kit) p. 209.

1.5-qt *Pyrex* Sculpted Loaf Pans with Covers

Again, we needed a specific size of glass loaf pan for use in the Beginner Section, as well as one that could also be used to house your Refrigerator Mother once you move into the Advanced Section. Its red plastic lid is easy to wash and works well for storage of your Refrigerator Mother.

8-cup *Pyrex* Measuring Cup

This is just the handiest thing ever because it functions as a mixing bowl *with a handle* when it comes time to give your batter a good stir.

5- to 6-qt Lidded Cast-Iron Dutch Oven

A lidded Dutch oven is needed to make our Beginner Dutch-Oven Bread on p. 46 in the Beginner Section and our Advanced Dutch-Oven Bread on p. 168 in the Advanced Section. We have a Dutch oven with a cast-iron interior, but an enameled interior will also work. Because of its heat-retention qualities, a cast-iron Dutch oven is necessary to create the kind of crisp, rustic crust that only cast iron can give.

Baking Parchment Paper

For lining pans to create a nonstick surface, and for sliding breads into the oven with ease, baking parchment paper sheets (16 1/2" x 12 1/4") from King Arthur Flour are our go-to choice. The reason we prefer this brand of parchment sheets over other sheets or rolls is because it has a maximum oven temperature of 450°F, while the maximum oven temperature for common parchment paper is 400°F. This is important because, in many of our recipes, breads are baked at 425°F.

Lasagna Trio Pan

This pan is ideal for making perfectly sized loaves for our Fruit & Nut Crackers on p. 54 in the Beginner Section.

1/8-cup Coffee Scoop

Plastic coffee scoops are easy enough to find, but we're in love with our handcrafted 1/8-cup scoop made by *Blue Prairie Kitchenware*. Because you feed your mother 3/8-cup flour, a coffee scoop makes more sense than telling you to measure out six tablespoons.

Silicone Spatulas

For giving our mothers a daily stir, we must admit we would rather use something carved from wood, so we sent our *Glasslock* bowl off to an artisan woodworker to see if he could fashion the perfect tool. What he sent back was a beauty, but while it matched the curve of the bowl on the bottom, it didn't match the curve of the sides. Not to mention, a wooden spatula wouldn't love being scrubbed with water twice a day. For maintenance of a mother, two good silicone spatulas work well, one for stirring and one for cleaning off the excess on your stir spatula. We like the silicone spatulas made by HeirloomLiving.us.

Flour-Sack Cotton Towels

Our choice for size (just the right amount of towel for tucking your mother in every night), durability, and absorbency measures 28" x 28". *Utopia Kitchen* offers a bleached cotton 12-pack and *ACS Home and Work* offers an unbleached 28" x 29" 12-pack.

Quick-Read Digital Thermometer

The economical thermometer made by *Taylor* is a great addition to any home kitchen and is especially useful for testing the internal temperature of breads. The downside is that it is comparatively slow, taking an average of 10 seconds to get an accurate temperature reading when inserted into breads.

Instant-Read Digital Thermometer

Thermoworks makes a sleeker, faster, albeit more expensive, kitchen thermometer. We tested two of their models. The ThermoPop is reasonably priced and comes in a wide array of colors. It reads temperatures almost instantly, taking an average of 3–4 seconds once inserted into bread. Another great benefit to this thermometer is that the probe is thin, so it doesn't leave a noticeable hole in breads after the internal temperature has been checked.

If you're looking for a great all-around fast and accurate kitchen thermometer, the Thermopen Mk4 is an excellent choice. Not only does it read temperatures quickly (an average of 2–3 seconds), it has a motion sensor that will turn the thermometer on when moved, and off when set down. Since the probe folds down, it's also easy to store. Depending on the angle at which you're holding the thermometer, the display screen automatically rotates, so you can read temperatures from any angle.

Norpro 8" x 4.5" Nonstick Bread Pan

Norpro pans are our favorite for baking breads because not only are their nonstick surfaces the best, they also leave a subtle waffle pattern on the sides of the loaves. This size pan is perfect for both our Brioche on p. 154, and our Bara Brith on p. 156 in the Advanced Section.

Norpro 10" x 4.5" Nonstick Bread Pan –OR–
Jamie Oliver 1.5-Litre Nonstick Loaf Tin

For making our Sandwich Loaf on p. 112 in the Advanced Section, you'll need either the 10" Norpro pan or the *Jamie Oliver* pan, which is heavier with a lovely light-blue finish.

Norpro

Jamie Oliver

USA Pan 13" x 4" Nonstick Pullman Loaf Pan and Lid

If you are making our Pain de Mie (Pullman Loaf) on p. 118 in the Advanced Section, you'll need this pan. This bread is baked in the pan with the lid on, to create a large, rectangular loaf that is browned on all four sides.

Mini Loaf Pans

If you are making our Pull-Apart Pumpkin Loaves on p. 162 in the Advanced Section, then you'll need four mini loaf pans. Each pan measures 3.75" x 5.5" x 2". A set of four mini loaf pans by *BIA Cordon Bleu* can be found online.

Oval Baking Tin (for gluten-free breads only)

This baking tin is essentially an adjustable, tall, oval ring. The *Westmark* Oval Baking Tin works extraordinarily well for helping our Gluten-Free French Breads on p. 80 in the Advanced Section hold their shape.

13" x 9" Glass Baking Dish

You will need a standard 13" x 9" glass baking dish for our Parker House Rolls on p. 132 in the Advanced Section.

7" Enameled Cast-Iron Dutch Oven

Adding ice cubes to a preheated, enameled cast-iron Dutch oven or an enameled cast-iron skillet that is at least 7" in diameter creates a blast of steam that adds moisture to the oven air during the first few minutes of baking to create a crisp, crackly outer crust on breads, while keeping the interior moist and supple. This step is critical on some of our breads in the Advanced Section because during the first few minutes a loaf is in the oven, it does a fair amount of rising (called "oven spring"). Adding moisture to the air enhances this rise. As the ice melts, creating steam, the added radiant heat from the baking stone and the enameled cast-iron Dutch oven or the enameled cast-iron skillet pitch in to help. For a more thorough explanation on why nothing but cast iron will work to create steam, see p. 216.

12" Cast-Iron Skillet

A cast-iron skillet is needed to make our Cast-Iron Skillet Bread on p. 122 in the Advanced Section. For this recipe, it's important to use a well-seasoned skillet; otherwise, the bottom and sides of your bread will discolor. If you're in the market for a new one, an enameled cast-iron skillet solves that problem.

If you want to know more about how to keep a non-enameled skillet "well-seasoned" (those two words we all dread), or how to revive or give renewed life to cast-iron bakeware in general, my book, *MaryJane's Cast Iron Kitchen,* has an entire section devoted to cast-iron care. Because it's a topic that's usually skirted around, or the seasoning oil that is recommended doesn't really work, I set out to make sure my cast-iron care tips were ... well, well-seasoned.

15"-Square Pizza Stone

A 15"-square pizza stone is used to mimic the effects of a masonry oven. Most notably, breads baked directly on the pizza stone cook evenly and develop a crisp crust. We prefer a square pizza stone over a round stone because with a round stone, long loaves such as our Bâtards on p. 62 or our French Bread on p. 76 in the Advanced Section that are baked directly on the stone would drop off the edges of a round stone. We use a *Pizzacraft* 15"-square pizza stone.

Pizza Peel

A pizza peel is an essential tool to have for quite a few of the breads in the Advanced Section. It's used to transfer loaves to and from the oven with ease. We prefer a pizza peel with a thin, metal blade rather than a thicker, wooden-bladed pizza peel because it's easier to slide the metal blade under loaves. We like the *Artaste* folding pizza peel with a 12" x 14" perforated blade.

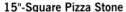

Baker's Linen, 24" x 36" (also called a Baker's Couche)

This heavy linen allows bread to breathe during rising, and at the same time, the stiff fabric helps the bread maintain its form. We use a *Breadtopia* 24" x 36" baker's linen.

Baguette Board

This handy board allows you to smoothly transfer baguettes (in our case, bâtards, ficelles, and epis) from your work surface to the baker's linen, and from the baker's linen to the baking pan. The beveled edge lets you get close to the bread and then roll it onto the board. We use a *Breadtopia* 24" x 4" x 1/4" Baguette Bread Flipping Board.

Bread Lame

A bread lame is essentially a razor blade connected to a handle. It's a great tool to have for slashing the tops of loaves before baking. A serrated knife can be used in place of a bread lame, but slashes made with a serrated knife aren't as clean and precise as those made with a bread lame. We love both the beauty and function of our black-walnut bread lame made by *Zatoba*. They even offer a left-handed version.

8"-Round Banneton Proofing Basket

This basket is used to make our traditional Boule on p. 70 in the Advanced Section, and is also used to help our Gluten-Free Dutch-Oven Bread on p. 170 in the Advanced Section hold its shape. Bread is not baked in the basket; it's used for shaping only. Before each use, the basket is generously dusted with flour. It does take a few uses to "season" the basket with flour. During this time, you might try dusting with a layer of tapioca starch before dusting with a layer of flour. After each use, lightly brush excess flour away with a brush. Water should never be used to wash a banneton basket. If you don't have a banneton basket, you can line a glass bowl that's 8–8 1/2" in diameter with a flour-sack cotton towel, generously dust the towel with flour, add dough, and proceed as the recipe directs.

Wooden Dough Scraper

A dough scraper is most commonly used for scraping stuck-on flour and dough from countertops after kneading breads. We prefer wood because metal dough scrapers tend to mar countertops. Even better, we like using a bread-dough cloth (p. 210) so our counters stay clean. It's also useful for stirring sprouted grains when drying, as seen in the Let's Talk Flour Section (p. 198), and comes in handy when we fold our Ciabatta dough on p. 100 in the Advanced Section. We like the *Kitchen Carvers* handmade maple dough scraper.

Bowl Scraper

A silicone bowl scraper is a great tool for removing sticky dough from bowls. In addition, it comes in handy for recipes that require the dough to be folded, like our Bâtard on p. 62 in the Advanced Section. We like the size and function of the *OXO Good Grips* 2-piece bowl-scraper set.

Stainless-Steel Skimmer

For making our Soft Pretzels on p. 144 in the Advanced Section, you'll want a stainless-steel skimmer on hand for removing the pretzels from the baking-soda water. It's large enough to cradle a pretzel without damaging its shape when scooping it out of the water. It also works for our Bagels on p. 140, and cake doughnuts on p. 184. We like the *Vollrath* 6 5/16" round-blade, stainless-steel skimmer.

Spray Bottle

A 4-oz spray bottle is used to spray the tops of rice-flour loaves with a water-and-baking-soda mixture to brown the tops of the loaves. We prefer a small spray bottle because it allows more control over the spray.

Put a spin on your bread making by incorporating a little pedal power. My Montana-made, hand-crank grain mill with bicycle conversion kit can be found at GrainMaker.com. I found the bike at a garage sale and painted it red to match the mill.

Specialty Equipment

Raadvad Guillotine Bread Slicer

Manufactured by a Danish company that dates back to the 1700s, these bread slicers were in production in the 1900s. These slicers are readily available from online vintage retailers in a variety of colors and conditions. This slicer is as much fun to look at as it is to use. When ours arrived, we couldn't wait to test it out on a crusty bâtard. It also cut our Fruit & Nut Crackers into beautiful, clean, even slices.

Bread Knife

The *Ronco* Sportsman Knife is the absolute best bread knife we've used. The thin, curved blade with wide serrations slices right through crusty and soft breads alike.

Kitchen Scale

A kitchen scale is very useful for dividing batter and dough into even portions. Our *Salter* High-Capacity Glass Scale is a kitchen workhorse. It has a 30-lb capacity and can toggle seamlessly between units of measure. In addition, it has a long battery life and uses 3 AAA batteries.

Bread Machine

We recommend the *Zojirushi* Home Bakery Supreme 2-lb Loaf Bread Maker for our Bread Machine Loaves on p. 164 in the Advanced Section. It's simple to use, easy to program, and a breeze to clean.

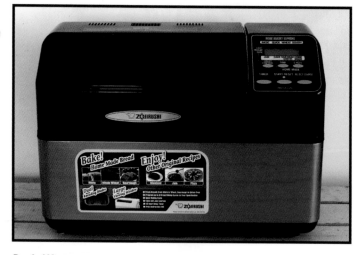

WonderMill Grain Mill

When it comes to milling specialty grains and seeds like rice or quinoa, we like our tabletop *WonderMill* the best. It doesn't create much dust and the milling chamber and fins are stainless steel, which helps keep the flour from overheating. It's easy to use and clean and comes with specialty attachments for things like quinoa, corn, amaranth, teff, and even coarse salt. If you're going to use it for anything other than wheat, make sure you buy the appropriate attachments.

Bee's Wrap

This stuff is the bee's knees for wrapping bread or to cover a bowl. It's reusable, lasts for about a year, and can be laundered. It's pliable and sticks to itself. Available in different sizes, you can use it to wrap loaves of bread, even sandwiches. Their 17" x 23" size will wrap any of our breads. Made from beeswax and cotton cloth, it comes in different, colorful designs.

Food Dehydrator

Like most kitchen appliances, food dehydrators for drying sprouted grains to make a wide variety of sprouted flours (p. 198) come in many sizes and shapes, with a wide assortment of features. Heating elements vary. Some are vented; some are not. Most have noisy fans that pull dust onto the food you're drying, but there's one exception. A woman named Gen MacManiman from Fall City, Washington, designed the perfect dryer in 1970, and started selling them in 1973. I purchased one of her models in 1980 for making healthy treats for my babies. I'm still using it today, along with three more countertop models and eight of her jumbo commercial dryers. Gen (short for Genevieve) passed away in 2011 at the age of 95, but her business and Gen herself were still going strong at age 89 when I called her to place an order. A dryer this good deserves to find a place in your kitchen. Gen's book, *Dry It—You'll Like It!*, published in 1974 and now out-of-print but available through some online sellers, includes plans for building her dehydrator.

Water Distiller

If you're looking to distill your own water at home, we like the *H2O Labs* Model 300 Water Distiller because it's so user-friendly. It has an all-stainless-steel boiling chamber and a glass carafe. The streamlined design makes distilling your own water at home as simple as filling the boiling chamber, lining up the carafe to catch the distilled water, and turning the machine on.

Water Purifier

I started purifying my water when I purchased my farm in 1986 because the original hand-dug homestead well that was here was shallow and tested high in nitrates, the result of surface water finding its way into the well. Since then, I've dug a much deeper well that tests negative for contaminants of any kind. To have your water tested, contact AnatekLabs.com. My choice for an under-counter purifier is the iSpring 6-stage, reverse-osmosis system with an alkaline remineralization filter. It filters 1,000+ contaminants, including chlorine and fluoride, and then reintroduces ionized minerals like calcium, magnesium, sodium, and potassium.

Bread Proofer with Shelf Kit

The *Brød and Taylor* folding bread proofer and yogurt maker is a versatile appliance that can house your Counter Mother if your average ambient room temperature is lower than 70°F. In addition, it can speed up rising times. For example, our Beginner Batter Bread recipes on p. 32 in the Beginner Section take 6–8 hours to rise in a warm place (70–73°F). The same bread, when placed in a proofer set to 85°F, will rise in 3–6 hours. When making Beginner Batter Bread, the added shelf kit enables you to fit both bakeware dishes into the proofer at once.

Old-Fashioned Countertop Guardian
(23" square)

You'll need:
basic sewing supplies
1 yard 9-oz canvas
shelf and drawer liner, cut to 22" x 22"

(Find canvas at your local fabric store or order online. Jo-Ann
Fabrics carries an 8.85-oz weight. I ordered organic cotton
canvas from OrganicCottonPlus.com and fell in love with its
texture, heft, and suppleness.)

1. Wash canvas in hot water and dry in your dryer on
   medium heat at least twice to fully shrink. Most canvas
   will lose 3"–6" in length, and 1"–2" in width.

2. Using the easy-to-follow weave of the canvas, cut out a
   23" square. (Don't use the selvage edge, because after
   you've shrunk the canvas, it will be rippled.)

3. Sew a 1/4" twice-turned hem along each side. Press flat.

4. To customize your gift, give it a touch of embroidery.

Place the cut piece of
shelf and drawer liner
under your cloth to keep
it from slipping around on
your counter.

Bread-Dough Cloth Gift Bag

(17" x 19")

This idea turns the cloth into a gift bag (your recipient can simply cut the twill tape off before use).

You'll need:
basic sewing supplies
1 yd 9-oz canvas
5 1/4 yds 5/8" twill tape
shelf and drawer liner, cut to 16" x 18"

1. Follow steps 1–3 (at the left) but this time, cut out a 17" x 19" piece of canvas.

2. On one of the 17" sides, 1" from the finished edge and centered, customize your gift by giving it a touch of embroidery.

3. Make side ties: Cut 4 pieces of twill tape, 14" each. Fold end of one tie over 1/4". Place with folded end down on the back side of the cloth, 5/8" from the corner along one of the long sides. Stitch along the fold of the twill tape and along the edge of the canvas. Repeat for other ties at each corner.

4. Make top ties/handles: Cut 2 pieces of twill tape, 48" long. On one tie, make a mark 13" from each end. Fold along each mark. Place one fold, short side up, 3 1/2" from the corner on one short end. Repeat for the other fold, making sure not to twist the handle in the middle. Stitch along the fold of the twill tape and along the edge of the canvas. Repeat for other handle. Angle-cut the ends of the twill tape and tie them in a knot.

5. Fold the top third down lengthwise and roll up the shelf and drawer liner and tie with a 32" length of twill tape, angle-cutting the ends. Put a *Wild Bread* book, a 5-lb bag of flour (a gallon ziplock bag holds 5 lbs of flour), and the liner in your gift "bag."

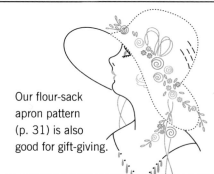

Our flour-sack apron pattern (p. 31) is also good for gift-giving.

shelf and drawer liner

Wild Bread

WILD BREAD

5 lb sack of flour

13" + 22" + 13" = 48" total

14" each

Local wheat farmer and poet Dick Warwick holds a precious memento given to him by Joseph.

The Old Meeting Hall

An old grange hall stands bereft
    In a field of waving wheat;
The people all have long since left,
    Where once with flying feet

They danced the fiddle's lively reels,
    And do-si-doed in squares;
But television and automobiles
    Have ended such affairs.

The neighbors all came from their farms
    For camaraderie;
From tiny newborn babes in arms
    To the deaf and doddery.

And they knew each other well, with all
    Their virtues, strengths, and faults;
They'd get together in the hall
    For the foxtrot and the waltz;

To share their pies and socialize,
    Talk of kids and kitchens—
Of critters, crops, and days gone by;
    Mark births and deaths and hitchin's.

For we were all one family then,
    Though perhaps not blood related—
Yes, I remember way back when
    We all cooperated.

We helped each other in a pinch
    Or sometimes just for fun;
If you needed help it was a cinch
    Your project would get done.

Though times back then were somewhat lean,
    Entertainment—it was free;
When folks would in that hall convene
    And friends and neighbors see.

And that old grange hall speaks to me
    Of things gone quite askew
In our present-day society
    With its hype and ballyhoo.

For folks now travel fast and far,
    Meet schedules with precision;
And when they're not out in the car
    They're watching television.

The art of actual conversation
    Is rather antiquated—
We've lots of information,
    But can't communicate it.

Oh, sure, we can download it
    And shift it place to place;
But there's few who can decode it
    Into words of style and grace.

So I miss the meeting hall of old,
    And I wish you could have known
How it was to cross the threshold
    Of that place, now overgrown,

And dance all night with the neighbor gal
    That you'd known since you were small;
Or meet your fated femme fatale,
    And in love forever fall.

Now that old building stands forlorn
    Yet still foursquare and sound;
Though by the wind and weather worn
    It could someday rebound,

For it hasn't yet been set aflame
    Nor from its footings torn,
And it may yet receive acclaim
    From dancers yet unborn.

So keep the roof in good repair
    And doors and windows sealed;
For past and future meet right there
    In that grange hall in the field.

        – by Dick Warwick, 1997

Bread making is an incredibly tactile, feeling-based, personal endeavor. While the recipes and methods throughout *Wild Bread* have been extensively tested, it's important to note that environmental and stylistic variables play a role in the end product. In an attempt to provide answers, offer solutions to common problems, and add a little bit of comfort and encouragement during your bread-making journey, here are the most common questions I've been asked over the years. Also, please join our network of home and professional bakers at WildBread.net, where all things *Wild Bread* are discussed.

But first, a note on the two types of mother referred to in this section:
• **Counter Mother** refers to the active mother you create in Section 1, **Beginner Breads**, p. 28.
• **Refrigerator Mother** is a fully mature mother that lives in your refrigerator with weekly feedings (and weekly Bake Days), Section 2, **Advanced Breads**, p. 58.

If the general term "mother" is used, it applies to both a Counter and Refrigerator Mother.

Q: The room temperature varies in my house. How cold is too cold?
A: A room temperature of 70–73°F is the ideal temperature range for your Counter Mother. If your house is colder than that or drafty or frigid because you set your air conditioning to 65°F in the summer, I recommend keeping your Counter Mother in a bread proofer (see Section 5, Equipment, p. 209) that is set somewhere between 70–73°F. If you keep your mother warmer than 73°F, she'll be more active; colder, she'll be less active. Let's say you lower your thermostat at night to 65°F but turn it back up into the 70s during the day. That will work, but if she's consistently kept at 65°F, she won't be as active as a 73°F mother. Also, the flour used to feed her and for bread making needs to be at room temperature.

Q: Which type of water is best?
A: Since water quality varies, I recommend using distilled water to get started creating and feeding a mother (in addition to adding water when making bread dough) while you figure out how to purify your tap water if you don't already. You can buy an under-counter purifier or a countertop water distiller (Section 5, Equipment, p. 209). For more about water quality, see p. 26. Also, the water used to feed your mother and for bread making needs to be at room temperature.

Q: Can I store my mother in a crock?
A: Our best method for success is the method described in detail on p. 28 and p. 58. Having exhaustively tested several methods that include storage in a crock (a method I used for many years), we decided that a glass see-through bowl in the exact size we recommend, covered with a cloth "lid" that allows your mother to breathe, fits our recipe volumes perfectly. Our method is the only one we can recommend with complete confidence. It makes caring for a mother an absolute pleasure.

Q: I just started my Counter Mother and I'm worried that it's too thick. Am I doing something wrong?
A: For the first couple of days, before the gluten proteins in the flour are broken down, your mother will be a little thicker. By the fourth day, your Counter Mother will be easier to stir.

Q: What should my Counter Mother smell like?
A: Your mother shouldn't really smell like anything other than flour and water paste for the first couple of days. As your mother begins to ferment (this usually starts on day 3 or 4), you'll begin to notice a light, tangy, fermented smell. By the end of the week, as Bake Day nears, your Counter Mother should have a pronounced "sour" smell, like a stout beer.

Q: How do I know if my mother is bad?
A: If your mother has any fuzzy black or red patches of mold, it shouldn't be used. Also, if your mother smells spoiled or unpleasant in any way, it's likely bad. If you have any reason to think that your mother has been contaminated by an accidental spill (it was sitting next to a spot where you prepared a messy meal using meat or raw eggs), it should be discarded. Once established and properly cared for, the acidic nature of a mother prevents bad bacteria from taking hold (the yeasts give off carbon dioxide, which causes bread to rise).

Q: Fruit flies are attracted to the towel covering my Counter Mother. How can I repel them?

A: During the warmer months, your mother might attract fruit flies. The handy fruit fly traps made by *BEAPCo* are more appealing to the flies than your mother is and work great when placed on the counter next to your mother. When they're full, simply toss the trap and start over with a fresh one. For a homemade version, pour some balsamic vinegar into a small bowl, put plastic wrap tightly over the top, and poke holes in it. Place it on the counter next to your Counter Mother.

Q: Before I feed my mother, I notice a layer of liquid on the surface. Is this normal?

A: Liquid on the top of your mother is a result of natural separation. If this happens to your Counter Mother, just stir it back in when you feed her. Once you're keeping a Refrigerator Mother, you'll have a more pronounced layer of liquid on the top of your mother at weekly feedings, and possibly some surface discoloration. As long as your mother continues to smell pleasantly sour, she's perfectly healthy.

Q: What if I can't bake bread the morning that my Counter Mother is ready?

A: If Bake Day rolls around and you're unable to bake bread, you can feed your mother as usual and bake bread that evening (you'll have a more voluminous mother). If you're unable to bake bread on Bake Day, you can divide your mother into ready-made, 1/2-cup portions for any of our sourdough-enhanced treats and freeze the portions for later use. In this instance, it's okay to freeze portions of your mother, because you won't be using it to give rise to bread, but to enhance the flavor and nutritive benefits of quick-and-easy things like pancakes, muffins, doughnuts, and chocolate cake that instead use baking powder for loft.

homemade fruit-fly trap

Q: What if I can't bake bread the morning that my Refrigerator Mother is ready?

A: If you have an established Refrigerator Mother, you can skip up to four consecutive Bake Days, as long as you continue with weekly feedings. Once you resume Bake Days, you can use up any accumulated mother in extra batches of breads, or you can divide your mother out into ready-made, 1/2-cup portions for any of our sourdough-enhanced treats and freeze the portions for later use. In this instance, it's okay to freeze portions of your mother, because you won't be using it to give rise to bread, but to enhance the flavor and nutritive benefits of quick-and-easy things like pancakes, muffins, doughnuts, and chocolate cake that instead use baking powder for loft.

Q: Do I need a special place to rise my dough?

A: That's the beauty of wild (naturally-leavened) bread versus factory yeast bread. The problem with factory yeast bread is it rises too fast, and consequently, if neglected, accidently bumped, or hit with a cold draft of air, it'll flatten fast, too, which is the reason some no-knead methods recommend rising bread in a refrigerator. Wild bread is incredibly forgiving. Of course, the warmer your room temperature, the faster your dough will rise. As a result, if your house is on the cooler side, your breads will take longer to rise. All the bread recipes in this book were tested in a room with a steady, average room temperature of 70–73°F. In quite a few of our recipes, we also utilized a bread proofer set to 85°F (see Section 5, Equipment, p. 209). We highly recommend a proofer. It takes away the uncertainty of variable temperatures and humidity.

Q: Why doesn't it seem like my bread is rising?

A: Perhaps the biggest adjustment to baking with wild yeast is the fact that the rise takes longer than for bread using factory yeast. If your mother is young, rising may be slow. The best way to gauge if your bread is starting to rise is to look at the surface of the bread. If there's activity on the top of the loaf such as air bubbles or stretch marks, your bread is rising. Depending on the conditions in your home, the first couple of Bake Days may produce slightly dense loaves. As your Counter Mother matures and pulls in more wild yeast from the air, your loaves will loft more, rising times will shorten, and signs of activity will be more obvious.

Q: How do I know if my bread has risen enough to bake?

A: In most of our recipes, visual cues are offered to help indicate when your bread is ready to bake. For example, our Sandwich Loaf recipe on p. 112 instructs you to bake your bread when it's level with the top of the pan. Although it seems like you would want to let it rise longer, it actually has a significant "oven spring," which means it will rise substantially in the oven.

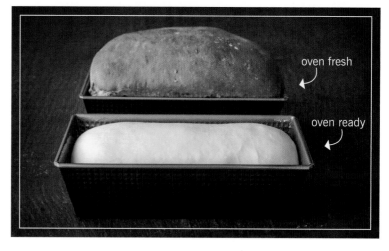

oven fresh

oven ready

Q: If my bread didn't rise after the first week, should I start a new Counter Mother?

A: No! Depending on the conditions in your home, your Counter Mother can take upwards of four weeks to pull in enough wild yeasts from the air to create a lofty rise.

Q: How do I know when my bread is finished baking?

A: If you want to be absolutely sure every time without fail, invest in a quick- or instant-read thermometer (see Section 5, Equipment, p. 203). To use one, you simply poke your bread (much like testing a cake with a toothpick) right in the center. If your bread has reached the temperature stated in the recipe and your crust is golden brown, it's finished baking.

Q: Why do several of the recipes in Section 2, Advanced Breads, call for adding ice to an enameled cast-iron Dutch oven or skillet? And why do I need an enameled cast-iron Dutch oven or skillet? Wouldn't any oven-safe pan work?

A: Adding ice cubes to a preheated, enameled cast-iron Dutch oven or an enameled cast-iron skillet creates a blast of steam that adds moisture to the oven air during the first few minutes of baking to create a crisp, crackly outer crust on breads, while keeping the interior moist and supple. This step is critical because during the first few minutes that a loaf is in the oven, it does a fair amount of rising (called "oven spring"). Adding moisture to the air enhances this rise. As the ice melts, creating steam, the added radiant heat from the baking stone and the enameled cast-iron Dutch oven or the enameled cast-iron skillet pitch in to help. The heat retention of cast iron is necessary to melt the ice quickly and create steam. An enameled surface on the pan is necessary because water isn't good for the surface of a traditional cast-iron pan. Because we were hesitant to recommend purchasing a pan solely for creating steam, we were determined to look for an alternative, and had the bright idea to place a pie tin inside the 12" cast-iron skillet you need for the recipe on our cover, with the hope that the skillet would transfer its heat to the pie tin and melt the ice quickly enough to produce steam. For our test, we placed a baking stone on the center oven rack, along with our enameled cast-iron 3.2-qt Dutch oven and cast-iron skillet/pie-tin combo side-by-side on the bottom rack and preheated the oven. Once the oven was up to temp, Ashley and I stood ready to add a cup of ice to both pans simultaneously and shut the door with the oven light on. Through the window, we saw the ice in the enameled cast-iron Dutch oven bubble and immediately create steam until it was gone, while the ice in the pie-tin-lined skillet barely started to melt and never did produce a blast of steam. For us, this justifies the need for an enameled cast-iron Dutch oven or an enameled cast-iron skillet. Keep in mind that any enameled cast-iron Dutch oven or skillet that's 7" in diameter or larger will work to create steam in your oven for baking breads. The one we use for steam came from a secondhand store and cost less than five dollars.

Q: What's the best way to store my bread?

A: Your bread will always be at its best right out of the oven (after cooling, of course), but unless you're feeding a crowd, you'll probably need to store it. Brown paper sacks work well if you're going to eat your bread within a day. Plastic bags will keep your bread moist for longer, but will also soften the crisp outer crust. For longer-term storage, put loaves into plastic bags and freeze (before they get too dry or too moist).

To prevent a damp crust after it's been in the freezer, remove your bread from its plastic bag and defrost it on a cooling rack. If you want to crisp the crust on your thawed bread, preheat oven to 325°F and place bread on a baker's sheet. Bake for 10–15 minutes, or until crust is crisp and bread is warmed throughout. For an alternative to plastic, try Bee's Wrap, p. 208.

Q: What if I'm going out of town?

A: Since it can take up to four weeks to get a Counter Mother established, it's important to start it when you're staying close to home. Once your Counter Mother is established and is ready to be converted to a Refrigerator Mother, you only need to feed it once a week. If you're going out of town for longer than a week, you can skip a single weekly feeding and your Refrigerator Mother will bounce back once you resume feedings. If you're going out of town for an extended period of time, you'll need to use up or discard your Refrigerator Mother and start a new Counter Mother once you return. Don't be tempted to put your mother in the freezer; this wreaks havoc with the wild yeasts and isn't something we recommend.

Q: Can I start a mother using your method, but use a packaged starter instead?

A: Although it may be tempting to purchase a sourdough starter with notability, fame, or an appealing exotic name, it's important to understand that a sourdough starter is a product of its environment. The minute you mix it with your own flour and water and the air in your home, it begins to adapt to its new environment. The same principle can also be applied to the concept of heirloom starters and years-old (even decades-old) starters. Since they're very much alive and you remove a large portion each week to bake with, your mother eventually "speaks a new language" altogether, based on location.

Q: Do I need a different mother for each kind of flour that I want to use?

A: Yes, because the volumes in our recipe charts are based on single-flour mothers.

Q: My bread is completely flat on the top with little to no definition. What happened?

A: Moisture in bread making has a large impact on the appearance of breads. Too much moisture, and breads will be ill-defined and flat. When you get the moisture just right, bread will rise and have clear definition in a multitude of different shapes. Alternatively, if you don't have enough moisture, bread will be dense and cakey. Once you get a feel for the whole process, getting the moisture just right will become second-nature. Use your best instincts—in most cases, you want your bread to be stretchy and pliable with just a little tack. If your bread dough is sticking to your hands, add a little extra flour or coat your hands lightly with cooking oil.

too much moisture

too dry

perfection!

... the original idea behind sourdough is that it's a leavening agent, why do the authors in my collection of bread books tell me to add baker's yeast? In addition, they tell me only white flour will work. And if they do use whole-wheat flour, they call for adding vital wheat gluten to the mix so the bread will rise. Is it possible to use 100 percent whole-wheat flour, or will my bread be dense and flat?

A. The term "sourdough," as it's used today, speaks more to flavor than to technique. Sourdough packets are usually a mixture of baker's yeast, dried acetic acid (vinegar—responsible for the sour "flavor"), and other natural or artificial ingredients. Sometimes, a sour flavor is accomplished by adding potatoes, grapes, or pineapple juice, or by letting dough made with baker's yeast rise overnight in the refrigerator. An authentic starter capable of giving rise to bread on its own is an ecosystem that is forever ONLY flour, water, and air. A stable, harmonious community composed of airborne bacteria and yeasts, the acidic nature of it prevents bad bacteria from taking hold and the yeasts give off carbon dioxide that causes bread to rise. If kept pure and taken care of properly, it will last forever with only the addition of more flour and water. And yes, it will give lofty rise to bread all on its own, even whole-grain breads, without the addition of white refined flour or vital wheat gluten, as are found in so many sourdough bread recipes.

Bread-book authors venturing into sourdough almost always end up wandering away from the authentic concept for bread-making-reliability reasons, even though they make their case for sourdough because …
It's the way bread has been made for thousands of years, ever since wheat was first cultivated, probably in the Fertile Crescent region of the world.
But what are the odds bread was invented the day someone's uneaten grain porridge sat in a bowl next to a fire all night, and the next day, full of bubbles, it fell into ~~the fire~~ a bowl of white, refined flour along with a packet of store-bought yeast? Historians think the term "sourdough" was introduced with the gold-rush days and miners' lack of kitchens and hygiene. In fact, miners were sometimes called "sours." Known for their campfire pancakes and overly vinegary starters that had a strong hooch (black, boozy liquid on top that was stirred back in before use), their crocks, no doubt, contained some pretty ripe ecosystems. I try to stay away from the term "sourdough" when it comes to bread. It's misleading, even though it's a term widely used in artisanal bread recipes. I do use the term to describe sour-flavored, panbread-type foods like pancakes made using a sour batter coupled with baking powder for loft.

My parents grew most of the food we ate. Not only did they feed us from the labor of their own hands, my father was a disciple of organic pioneer Robert Rodale, so the food we grew was also organic. When I left home and attempted to make a living selling organic food, I soon realized I would be ponying up a small fortune every year obtaining my organic certification, along with untold layers of inventory bookkeeping if I wanted to legally call my food "organic." Early on, I thought, "Why can't my carrots be called simply 'carrots' and non-organic, chemically produced carrots be called 'chemical carrots'?" Instead of me listing all the things I don't use, how about them listing all the things they do use to produce carrots? Anyway, I digress, but you get the idea. The term "Wild Bread" is my attempt to set myself apart from sourdough and the myriad ways in which it's been characterized and marketed. My formula puts a bread "starter" where it belongs, as a "mother" used to spawn bread, and yes, even single-flour, whole-grain bread, including gluten free. If sour is what you want, your bread needs a long, slow rise in a cool environment. If a loaf of soft, classic sandwich bread is what you're after, your mother wants nothing more than to see you rise to the top of your class. If you nurture a mother correctly and give her time to fully mature, she will loft bread for you the-way-nature-intended with all the rise you could ever want.

Q. What is it?

A. The purpose of the piece of mill equipment behind our bistro table in the group photo on p. 221 is speculation on our part. It was tucked into storage in a corner of our historic mill, so we brought it to the farm because it's too beautiful not to be admired daily. We think it's a sorter or grader (as in quality), most likely used for peas or maybe wheat. When peas traveled down the spirals, they were separated by velocity and gravity specific to the seed. The heavier ones would follow a different path than the lighter ones and end up in a different spiral on the way down, and eventually, a different container. Because peas damaged by weevils have their insides hollowed out by developing larvae, they would be a different weight than undamaged peas. Same thing with wheat that's been damaged by smut: it would travel at a different speed.

My ability to author a book has everything to do with those who help me. In this case, it has everything-but-the-kitchen-sink to do with my daughter-in-law, Ashley Ogle, who baked her heart out with me, at one point filling an entire freezer with the breads she'd created. (That was after we'd handed out bread to everyone who lives and works here at my farm.) When I launched the idea for *Bread the MaryJane Way* in 2008, I certainly didn't think it would take 10 years to turn my idea into a consistent, simplified set of blueprints. Thank you to my book team, staff photographers/graphic designers/sketch artists Karina Overfelt and Cydnie Gray; my daughter, Megan Rae, for content editing; Carol Hill and Priscilla Wegars for copyediting; and also to my dairyhands, Connie Dehlin and Julie Hopper; and my four granddaughters, who pitched in for kitchen duty and gave us child-approved feedback on everything we baked.

INDEX

ABOUT THE AUTHOR

Lessons gleaned from MaryJane Butters' diverse pioneering background, from carpenter to dairy owner to former wilderness ranger turned organic farmer, led her eventually to stewardship of the four-story, historic Barron Flour Mill. It was only natural that her years spent living in remote Forest Service outpost cabins and fire-watch towers with only a living, breathing, sourdough "mother" for companionship would lead her to write a pioneering wild-yeast bread book. She is the author of eight books; editor of *MaryJanesFarm* magazine, now in its 18th year of publication; and lives on an organic farm in Idaho. Two of her grown children and their spouses live and work full-time at her farm and she is "Nanny" to half a dozen grandchildren.

NOTES